Imaginationland

A Self Help Book

By

Aaron Wayno

September 2013

ISBN: 978-1-304-41627-8

Table of Contents

<u>Imaginationland</u>

Give your parents a bloody nose.

Steal their car and drive until it runs out of gas.

Leave it on the side of the road for the man with the gas can.

Find a bright patch of toadstools in a forest clearing.

Stay away from the brick red spider webs.

Follow the mosquitoes' nose all the way to the grass lands.

Prepare for a journey by gathering supplies. (Big stick, handful of summer huckleberries, chewing gum)

Walk through the thickets and watch them grow.

At first it is easy,

then it gets thicker,

and thicker,

until it becomes the thickest of the thickets!

Then you go from hard, to simple, in the blink of an eye.

The floor opens wide.

The grass stalks grow beyond your sight.

And when you are ready, the journey will go up.

Up.

Up.

Up.

Up, Up, UP.

To the unknowing lands in the sky.

To the tip, where the man with the troll bone necklace lurks.

Enjoy the laughter of the purple/green hummingbirds.

Help the blue bees on their secret mission.

Challenge a red bear to a Game of Jacks.

But beware the man with the troll bone necklace.

A black and white conjoined witch will give you advice.

No one will think less of you if you refuse their assistance.

An indifferent unicorn sleeps under an origami windmill.

A marathon party of ginseng roots runs across your path.

Some of them do cartwheels.

Some of them bow low.

Some of them have bloody heels.

One of them is named Joe.

A Pig in a Box and Fig with some Phlox deceive Joe while he runs.

You barely escape leave Joe to his fate to boil between the suns.

A knight comes along, with his silver throng accusing you of fail.

They gobble you up, steal your turnip, and throw you into jail.

The jail is filled with jolly, naked folks.

There are no cells.

No bars.

No clothes.

No guards.

Once a day a wooden cart parks outside the high walls and hurls food over the sides.

The prisoners gather the supplies.

Expired Jars of Human Honey and Fairy Jam.

Bags of Fly Manure.

Millions of loose Dandelion Seeds.

An Underfed Gelded Clydesdale with a twisted ankle.

Three French Hens. (Oui, Oui, Oui)

And dozens of tiny green apples, big as a newborn baby fists, sweet as pickled rhubarb.

Together with your help, the other prisoners, Hare the Rabbit, Steve the Magician, and Mike the Antique Watering

Can will create a working, functioning, breathing eco-system in the jail.

You will find wonder in the growing of apple trees.

In the jarring of jams.

In the attraction of bees.

In the digging of earth.

In the creation of compost.

In the prayers for rain.

In the celebration of success.

In the laughter of failure.

And just when you are content in your new home, with your new family, with all of your creations around you.

A door in the wall appears.

One that has been there the whole time.

And you have to decide.

If you want to stay and keep building what you have started.

Or go on out the door.

Or down the well.

That used to be deep and dark.

But now has a bright light.

Like that of a steam locomotive or a Christmas star.

Shining up at you from below.

Into something brand new.

<u>Dreaming About Souls</u>

Last night a woman made out of dreams and legends entered my soul. She arrived, swimming through mid air, floating on her back. She tread like a jellyfish and spoke to the rivers. "Let yourself feel the river my son." "The flow is all around us, if you let it." "Won't you join me?" Then I began to rise. I slowly slipped down stream, the soft warm covers of my bed slid from around my body to the earth, and I transformed from solid, to liquid, to Universe.

Couple in a Cafe

The couple sits in the corner of the fancy seafood restaurant, absorbing the silent glances of the wait staff, the chefs, the other customers in the booths, at the tables, in the bar and those still waiting to be seated.

The man with his long hair pulled back into the pony tail has the young woman with the dark pixie haircut and the glowing star skin shining in a full grin. Alternating from giggles to kisses to gratitude to longing gazes from one second to the next, the man looks as content as any king or newlywed husband or championship poker player. The woman looks sexy as hell. Like a sleek animal, a gorgeous fox on the casual prowl at night, a genius wide eyed owl spreading the word, or a bright white cat, the envy of every ordinary tom and stray in the alley.

They sit together and he orders their food without her knowledge. A game they like to play. When it comes, a bowl of clam chowder, a house salad, a shrimp appetizer, and a brownie with ice cream is set down before them. The man insisted to the waitress that all items be brought at the same time. A cornucopia of wonder and flavors! All at once!

The celebration of food and laughter and bliss radiates across the restaurant. Some people are encouraged by the energy. Others scowl at the display of genuine love. Affection and attraction that is so obviously lacking in their own lives. If their attitudes were different then there could be an opportunity for growth. An opportunity for evolution. It still might happen. Maybe some people grow much better when obvious examples of joy and magic are laid out before them. Maybe, later that night, a transformation will take place.

Maxine's Tale

When Maxine was a young girl, she lived in a one room shack in the middle of an enchanted forest. Every day her father would leave Maxine at home while he went to work at the hand grenade factory. She would spend her days singing and dancing all day long to the greatest pop hits of the nineteen eighties. Blondie, Cyndi Lauper, Madonna, Van Halen, Michael Jacksons "Thriller" was one of her favorites. She loved mimicking/perfecting the choreographed dance moves from the music video.

One day, during a vigorous rendition of Billy Idols "Dancing With Myself" She bumped the accidental table where the Dr. Suess goldfish sat in his rickety glass bowl, thinking his goldfish thoughts. It fell from the accidental table and exploded on impact. The water spread out like the Universe, then slowed, then crawled to a halt, all the while the goldfish flipped and flapped in the puddle, its silent gasping for air suddenly speaking to Maxine with the voice of God.

"Leave this place Maxine. Leave this glass bowl. Go see something. Anything. As long as it is something you have never seen before."

"I am sorry I kilt you."

"It's okay. I was tired anyway. This way I get to be what freedom feels like. If only for a few seconds."

The goldfish flapped two more times then fell still and stiff. Maxine left the cottage and the forest and did as the goldfish said. She thumbed a ride to Middle America and saw the food that feeds the whole world. From there she took train rides to seas and mountain tops. She flew to foreign countries. Saw the basement in the Eiffel tower. Breathed the scent of the Sistine chapel. Drank the bottled water at Lourdes. Punt kicked a hole in the Berlin Wall. Pissed off of the Great Wall of China. Found a time machine and traveled backward to about the time we were on our way to the moon.

Embrace Carrying Infinity Around

There are 200 billion stars in our own galaxy, and 200 billion galaxies in the Universe. And it just keeps on growing. So when I say that those two numbers when multiplied by each other come to a microscopic figure that accounts for only a tiny little piece of the infinity that is inside of each and every one of our brains, I hope you can try to understand the meaning of the word infinity.

Each one of us, for the blessed micro facture of existence we are given on this Earth, carry infinity around with us at all times. The infinity is the thing inside us where anything is possible. It is a place of magic and of wonder and of joy. It is a place of terror and of worry and of creativity and of judgment and of peace and of forgiveness and of a countless array of adjectives that have not even been invented yet. This infinity, this endless ability to create things and worlds and Universes and ideas and magic is boundless. There are things in the world that literally were not even a thought 100 years ago, fifty years ago, ten years ago, one year ago. Then out of nothing BAM they appear. The thought has a root, or two, it sprouts, it spreads, it grows, it breeds, with the help of buzzing bees, similar thoughts spring up around it. It is organic and natural. It is our infinite brains at work. Making magic for each other. Making magic for ourselves. Making magic for the Universe.

I guess the whole story comes down to who is positive

and who is negative. Is the glass half empty? Or half full? Is the glass overflowing, runnething over onto the table? Or is the glass empty, available to fill up with anything we want to. Or we can shatter the glass and go get a huge bucket, a huge tank filled with beautiful women, men in Speedos, exotic fish, public speakers beware. Smash the fucking glass. Fill your life with anything you want.

Use your infinity. Use the genius that you were endowed with by God. Become the image that he created you in.

People like to say, and I heard this quote when I was a little kid, that we only use ten percent of our brains. Jeez, ten percent? It seems like we are using ten percent and it is shrinking. I always aim for eleven percent. Twelve percent, thirteen percent. Every night I do my best to sink into parts of my brain I have never been to before. Parts that have been covered up with education, mathematics, tabloid T.V. reality T.V. Purge these mind rotting tools, in use to keep you out of your element, out of your genius, out of your evolutionary rights. Your right to enjoy your human experience the way God wants you to. God is not interested in you sitting on the couch and wasting away during manufactured television programs. God is interested in seeing you come before him as the most perfect person you can be. No human is perfect. No God is perfect. No universe is perfect. Thankfully, humanity was endowed with this wonderful tool. This wonderful brain. To try and make the impossibly high standard of perfection, possible. Thank you.

Carnivore in a Vegans Belly

I put a carnivore in a vegan's belly. It took us a while to realize this. We were worried at first. All of her favorite foods and super foods were suddenly being rejected by her body. Hummus, avocados, pomegranates, brown rice stir fry, broccoli, apples, morels, blueberries, strawberries, bananas, all led to a colorful cascade of bile and vomit. We went to the doctor, she was getting thinner, not bigger and he thought that she should change her diet. Try something that the baby feels like it might want. We left the office and I had the windows down when we drove through a neighborhood of manufactured homes. A scent wafted around the car and entered our midst. The vegans' eyes swelled like the Incredible Hulks. They grew wide and bloodshot; she was slavering and wanting to know what the orgasmic smell was. She has been a vegan since she was a baby, so I told her that she smelled barbeque, probably hamburgers and chicken. We followed the cartoon scent to where a bunch of cars were outside of one house. Turns out it was a wedding reception. We got out and crashed our way inside. There were tons of people there so we walked up to the cake, saw their names, Sean and Baby were the bride and groom. We went to the grill where a large man with a big smile was scorching half pound buffalo patties. By now the vegan was about to stab someone in the heart to get at one of those burgers. I got one for each of us and she attacked that hamburger like Cool Hand Luke in a boiled egg eating contest. I had about a quarter of my hamburger eaten when she ripped it out of my hands and devoured the rest of it. For a lark I walked over to the buffet table and looked at what else they had. It was like a meat eater's heaven. I grabbed my girl and together we had parts of: Bacon wrapped scallops, Bloody Prime rib, Kosher Hot dogs, King Crab legs, Seafood stew, Sheppard's pie, deep fried cheese stix, cottage cheese, goat cheese, cream cheese and salami on crackers, deviled eggs, teriyaki chicken, biscuits and gravy, chicken fingers, smoked salmon eyes, even lutefisk and tripe. We did not touch the grapes or the fruit salad, or the potato salad. We stood off to the side, observing and commenting on the people at this wedding, safe guarding the food on the plates I held while my vegan gave nourishment to the Tyrannosaurus Rex in her womb. He must have been in ecstasy as he engorged himself on the proteins and fats of a dozen different animals at once.

Carrie Coconuts

Carrie Coconuts was the worst babysitter of all time. She also doubled, tripled and homered as the first woman who I ever saw naked. The first woman I saw use drugs. And the first person I saw hit someone in the face.

She spent most of the babysitting time in the bathtub. Which was fine by us because when she was in there she could not threaten us or keep us from snooping around in drawers or the fridge. I wasn't even sure why she was there. She spent almost the whole night in the bathtub. It was a Jacuzzi tub that cost my parents 5000 dollars to install. And she spent about 95 percent of her time soaking when she was supposed to be watching us.

She was foul mouthed, and mean and she would say things like: "Okay you little shit machines. I am going to take a bath. If you make me get out you are gonna fuckin' eat it." Then she would climb in, lock the door and hit the jets for about two hours.

Once, I needed to get the baby pliers from the bathroom so I knocked on the door and no one answered. I pushed my way in and there was Carrie Coconuts laying in the tub. She had tiny rabbit titties. No hair between her legs. Her eyes were closed. I moved over and grabbed the pliers from the junk drawer and she goes, without opening her eyes, What are you doing.

And I go, "Pliers" I hold them out so she can see. Exhibit A.

She looks at me then, and she slurs all slow like a drooling dragon, do you 'anna fuck me?

I tell her that I am ten and she is all like, get out fuggin baby dick faggit.

I am about to run when she lifts her hand out from the water. She is holding my brothers eppy pen and I think that she is going to kill me or herself with it. But then she starts to stab the side of the tub and rant, Little Fucker, stop damaging my calm, get over here. It looks like she is stabbing hallucinations but then I see she is trying to kill a ant, which we have had in that bathroom since we moved in.

And not one of those tiny little adorable CGI ants you see on Pixar TV. Or carpenter ants, those kings of meandering aimlessly. These are mean, fast little bastards. With red heads and pinchers. It took her like five tries to stab it. But eventually she succeeds and holds it out, all skewered and wiggling and panicky, to show off.

What are you doing?

Sending ants to hell. Watch this. Then she says goodbye, and slides the tip of the syringe along with the ant into the flame of a candle that is burning by the tub. The ant is all curled and torched and a tiny puff of soul smoke appears above the flame and it is over before I can blink. See you later, she says to the ant, wiping what is left of the critter on the wet waxy edge of the candle. She starts looking around the tub for anything else that she might torch and murder for a milliseconds worth of amusement. Her eyes fix on me and I do not wait around long enough to find out what angle the devil is working in that rotten brain of hers.

Emy in the Forest

Sunlight filters through the tops of trees down to the bright green moss below. The boughs and branches sway slowly back and forth leisurely from a gentle northern breeze. The unrest above is almost enough to absorb the sounds of soft footsteps travelling unseen along the forest floor.

The child's small feet, bare, and sticking out from beneath the dirty white hem of a light blue dress were moving steadily along; careful not to step on any sharp sticks or rocks. The birds chirped in random and content happiness. The leaves spoke, rustled, and shook in their own way, without the assistance of wind. The footsteps of the child seemed to keep the beat. The sound of a girl humming quietly to herself joined in the ongoing symphony created by the natural world.

At that moment in a spot where the sun had managed to peek through all the way to the moist earth below, a mushroom pops up from the moss and grows up rapidly right in the middle of the young lady's path. Just as she was 'bout to step on it, her feet halt in the nick and observe for a moment. She could see it growing. Without help of rain it blossomed and unfolded wider and wider. Its orange tincture shining brightly in the light of the sun.

Emy pulled her knife from the pocket in the front center of her dress and tried to open it with one hand. Having seen her father do this hundreds of times she has not yet been able to master this trick. She gives up and uses two hands to pull out its dull steel edge. She sits down on both knees and puts her face within inches of the fungus placing the edge of the knife its base. A quick sawing motion and she will have her pot of organic fleshy gold.

Just then the sound of a man's heavy footfall comes echoing through the bushes. Rustling and thudding through the forest. Slowly; deliberately. The noise was moving slowly toward her as she remained kneeling and quiet, waiting for a chance to get a better look at who or what was approaching.

A Short List of Some Things I Have: September 6th 2006

I have ears. I have perspective. I have respect. I have life. I have soul. I have dance moves. I have the funk. I have a girlfriend. I have a job. I have a journal. I have lost almost 50 pounds. I have faith. I have passion. I have two married parents. I have 3 living grandparents. I have one brother. I have a great place to live. I have a great country to live. I have a good supervisor. I have vision. I have heart. I have a lot of love to give. I have a big fat cock. I have strange toes. I have a book club. I have a summer birthday. I have seen God. I have strange dreams. I have the Seattle Seahawks. I have vacations. I have a bass guitar. I have graduated high school. I have slowed down. I have had sex. I have given oral pleasure to a woman. I have been called many names. I have a chainsaw. I have friends. I have lost friends. I have been sick. I have had surgery. I have played sports. I have learned to swim. I have library fingers. I have written journals. I have drawn pictures. I have taken pictures. I have pissed people off. I have had road rage. I have been in an accident. I have hit a deer. I have been in a wedding. I have thought about killing myself. I have a great life. I have masturbated. I have been in a fight. I have been afraid. I have caused fear. I have been a wizard. I have flown a kite. I have had a cat. I have hit a homerun. I have tackled Tim Douglas. I have slam dunked a basketball. I have blocked a slam-dunk attempt. I have played wiffleball. I have played wall ball. I have been to the ocean. I have been Hitler. I have been a shit. I have been redeemed. I have helped people out of selflessness. I have helped people out of selfishness. I have rescued moths. I have killed many earwigs. I have stepped on ants. I have fed bugs to spiders in spider webs. I have gotten lost at Disneyland. I have written well tonight. I have indecision. I have many things to look forward to. I have books to read.

Move Along, Move Along

When I was a baby, I was dropped out of the window of a VW bus, right on my head. On my way to the hospital, my parents stuffed me into a cardboard box underneath the back seat. They could hear the scratching of my tiny fingernails on the cardboard over the rattle of the ancient diesel engine. Even though my head looked like a dented beer can, I did not cry.

My Dads Tears Taste Like Absinthe: they got pills for that

The Giant Penis rose out of the ocean then crashed down in the water like a failed space shuttle launch.

My stained glass father started to cry. It sounded awful. Like Redwood trees falling down. Like a terrorists test practical joke.

"God, just cry a little bit every once in a while and you won't have this problem."

But people don't know how to cry anymore cuz they got pills for that.

They got pills for everything. Seeing the future. Making babies. Not making babies. Time Travel. Automatic A's in Shop Class. Winning at Blackjack. Getting into Heaven.

He usually writes away his tears. He sits in the bubble bath and waits for the words to appear; like visions in the bubbles.

Sometimes they come. Most times he spaces out and drops the pen and papers in the water. He wakes up sixteen hours later freezing cold. With greasy wrinkly pimply chicken skin. Fingernails pale and luminescent like the inside of oyster shells. His penis shrunken down to the size and shape and color of an albino acorn.

<u>Wild Animals, Wild Mushrooms, Wild Minds</u>

There is something magical about the natural world. A world that celebrates life and love. A world that invites us to experience the wonder of the Universe. A world of chirping crickets, mating frogs, flourishing wildflowers, uncut grass on your bare toes, swimming in the ocean, watching clams squirt sea water three feet in the air, watching a family of bald eagles soar in circles without flapping their wings, watching a couple of crows snack on a deceased possum, drinking from puddles, naked bodies, orgasms, hair, play, teeth smiling, deep breathing, sandy beaches, the surface of the moon, the rays of the sun, organic vegetables, wild animals, wild mushrooms, wild minds.

The Hunted Man

You will be saved from the scorpions tucked away in the folds of his face.

The Hunted Man will fly in and rescue you.

He will teach you everything he knows.

By the firelight, your lessons reach their pinnacle.

Your lives disappear into the flaps of the Universe.

And the Hunted Man's pursuers remain at bay.

While swimming in the salt water you see a waterlogged stinging insect barely alive.

Your hands scoop from underneath

The water drains out.

His legs grab hold of the sudden solidification beneath him.

He crawls, with what little strength he has left.

You walk across barnacles toward the blackberry vines.

He climbs onto a leaf and begins to clean the saltwater out of the black and gold insect fur.

Later on, in the cold pools of the endless ocean. A giant the same shape as you scoops you up and walks you over. You saved your own life. Proof of Gods existence. Proof of warlocks and cyborgs in the world. So much joy and genius abounds. So much to soak up and be amazed by.

Cracks in the skin. Bugs in the folds of the old man's face. Monsters appearing through magnification. Watch out for Magnification Boy. He can see deeper and deeper into things. He can see molecules. He can see at sub atomic levels. He can see smaller and smaller until his chest hurts and his heart freezes. He has to close his eyes and look away. His eyesight returns to normal. His head is abuzz with old fashioned TV static. He uses old TV static to show kids what it looks like. "Put your face right up to this static," he says "and see if you can stand it."

Criss-Cross-Applesauce

She sat on the floor of the library criss-cross-applesauce reading books about sewing, about detoxifying foods, a picture book about a tractor saving farm animals from a tornado, a work of biographical fiction about a little girl growing up during the dustbowl, enduring the hardships of abuse from family and farm life in mid America during that time. She thought back to painting her boyfriends toenails. Scarlett Slippers. She sat the same way then, the tiny brush gliding across his thick toenails with adroit certainty. Chatting idly about the old days. About summer swimming in lakes, and walking up Indian trails to Boulder Cave, then following the river back down, munching on wild berries and feeling the cold slippery polished river stones beneath their pale near frozen feet. A line at the fanny slide, a line up at the Dexter's for soft serve and sno-cones. Back before the days of Cable T.V. and cellular phones and video cassette tape players with hi-speed dubbing.

Imaginationland: The Scientist
A Tale of Two Kitties

There was once a great scientist who lived in an abandoned missile silo. He created many wonderful things in his workshop. He constructed fine meals and iced creams. Including the best tasting Prime Rib and Goo-Goo- Cluster that had ever been invented. He taught a tree about motion and balance so that it could climb out of its flower pot and dip its roots into the bathtub or drinking fountain. He made a microchip that he installed just behind the ear of a black stray cat so he could hear the kitties thoughts. However, it had the added unexpected bonus of creating communication between the two, so they had many conversations and he taught the cat new and useful things. How to use a can opener. How to program an alarm clock so he would stop sleeping through important business, like finding girl cats. And he taught the cat about his own mortality and the slow approach of death. Which was something that, after the fact, he regretted doing. But the cat was a good sport and seemed fine with this knowledge and it gave him the chance to face death, and to make the honorable choice of defiance. They quickly became best friends and the cat and the scientist began work on even smaller more complicated machines, small enough to be contained in the blood of a human or plant or animal. To help boost immune systems, increase speed and balance and to choose your best temperature. If it was cold the machines could warm you. If it was hot they would make things comfortable again. They were connected to the brain in a way that helped to choose which ailments you wanted them to work on. They formed cures for everything from wrinkly skin to bad eyesight, to back hair removal, to the elimination of viruses clogged arteries and cancers. The scientist used these machines on himself to become fit and young again. And when he discussed using them on his best and only friend, the stray cat, the cat after much deliberation and debate with his friend, refused. He told the scientist that to use the tiny machines would deny himself the greatest adventure, deny himself the answers to the mysteries of the soul and access to the great beyond, and to the fulfillment of final sleep. And to do all these things, would be bankruptcy indeed.

.

The Scientist listened to the stray cat and at first was astounded, then he slowed down and disappeared into a state of reflection and meditation. He focused on the things that the cat had held up so high. Mystery of the Soul, Adventure, The Great Beyond, Fulfillment, Final Sleep. During this time, the stray cat taught himself how to read and do back flips and how to attach and remove a collar. The scientist emerged from his reverie many weeks later and started work on a time machine. Using the natural spin of the Earth and the backward confluence of dreams and several other unlikely ingredients, a microwave oven, used motor oil from a vehicle made before 1970, volcanic glass, ice from a glacier, pop rocks; his machine was finished and ready to test. His friend, the cat, was eager to try it out. He was outfitted with a special collar that was intended to return him to the future after a preset amount of time. The cat climbed into the microwave oven and curled into wary kitty position. The scientist turned the knob and the microwave whirred as if cooking a chicken dinner with brownie. The cat's instructions were to fall asleep, and after this occurs, when he wakes up he will have arrived at his destination in the past.

The scientist watched eagerly as the cat sat in the old microwave. At first he thought it was not going to work. Who could fall asleep in a humming microwave? But the cat, for all his newfound knowledge, was a cat, and was accustomed to sleeping 20 hours a day. And soon simply from the act of curling into a kitty ball, he nodded off and the scientist watched as the cat disappeared without smoke, or sparks or fanfare. The time machine was a success.

Now the cat's collar was set for a three day journey. It was the longest three days of the scientist's life. He wished he had only made it a couple of hours, or at least one day, or that he been able to program the collar to return moments after the cat had left. He missed his friend, and began to worry, began to wonder, about what he would do, if something were to go wrong.

Finally the three days were up. And the scientist was in front of the microwave with a can of cat food waiting for his friend. Eager for his companionship and the stories of his adventure. The moment arrived and the microwave switched on of its own accord. Did the chicken dinner humming thing again and a cat appeared. It was in a panic, thrashing and trying to get out of this tiny enclosed space it suddenly found itself in. The scientist opened the door and a white fluffy female with pink ribbons in her fur leaped out and darted underneath a cot. The scientist eventually coaxed her out with a bowl of replica tuna fish, and once she was out he studied her. She was clearly beset with fear, shaking all over, unable to speak or understand a word of English, and wearing his friend, the stray cats, time travel collar.

The scientist did what he could to help the poor kitty but she was inconsolable. He even installed a chip behind her ear so he could communicate with her but she was too racked with worry and an urge to flee that he could gain no further understanding of what had happened. He had only his theories and scientific hypothesis to guide him.

The scientist became overcome with guilt and sadness, blaming himself at the loss of his friend. He started to focus on what he could to do correct his error. He started to dabble in genetic experimentation. Attempts to use proteins and amino acids to build new life, and new life forms took all of his time. After many failures and abominations, he finally gained a little bit of traction making a small three limbed ginger shaped bipedal life form that had no head and spoke an indecipherable brand of English through a mouth where the fourth limb should have been. It was close enough for the scientists needs. He cloned many of these creatures all of which were named "Glor" and sent them through the time machine, each with a replica collar that would return the stray cat back to his present time if they found him and could attach the collar properly. The Glor were constructed without a soul, to build a soul for each Glor was way too complicated and time consuming. Their life spans were only about 52 hours, so the scientist was not at all self conscious about sending these genetic beings into the past to do his bidding.

For months, the scientist made calculations and tried to send the Glor back in time to the precise moment that he had sent The Stray Cat. He tried to figure out where and when he could reach the cat if the cat had continued on his path through its timeline in the past. The scientist was despondent over the lack of success. He spent most of his time laying in bed barely enough energy to eat and drink, only getting up to feed the white female cat, who spent most of her time hiding under his mattress.

One day the scientist, feeding the timid white lady cat, thought she looked unusually plump around the belly. He gave her an examination and quickly determined her to be filled with a soon to be delivered litter. He did all he could to help her make a nest that would be comfortable. Basket, soft blankets, lots of tuna and milk extract. A good seat in Heaven. Then one day she disappeared under the mattress and would not come out. The scientist, for once, did not interfere. He let the white kitty do her thing. Allowed her to give birth and when the yowling ended she sat with the small group of kittens. One black, one white, one black and white striped, one white with a black tail, one black with white paws, one black and white spotted like a moo-moo cow.

After the kittens were born the scientist dismantled the time machine, his equipment for nano-probes and his Glor cloning apparatus. He turned his laboratory, the old missile silo into a cat nursery, his inventing reduced down to improve the diet and foodstuffs of the litter, to making the white kitty with the pink ribbons in her fur as comfortable as possible, and to building the best toys and games of amusement that any cat had ever seen in the history of kittens.

Refuse to Choose Ordinary:
And the Liberty of Forgetfulness

Sometimes I forget. There was that great comparison in Neverwhere. The best part of the book was the last part. When all he really wants to do is to go back. To have a "normal" life again. But he saw that ordinary does not work for him anymore. Ordinary is hard to deal with. It is like, do you want to have a regular job? Or do you want to have your best life. It is a book about choosing your best life. It is a story about deciding what the best thing is for you. There was a moment when he is describing waking up and forgetting who he is. One of the most frightening feelings that someone over the age of forty can succumb to. Forgetfulness. Waking up, and realizing you have forgotten who you are, and deciding that this means that the world is laid out before you. You can become a seagull and fly to the sea. You can become a king of a faraway land, in distance and time. You can become a star. You can become a child again. You can live under the sea and between the stars. You can do-have-be-want-think-own-live-love anything you want. That is a wonderful place. Sometimes when you are awake forgetfulness takes over. The blessed liberty of forgetfulness. The peace. Being reminded is hard sometimes. Even harder for the reminder. I have a wonderful life. I am so glad to be me. I am so glad that I am here and now. I am a wonder and a joy to behold. I love my words. I love my brain. I love my Universe. Peace lads. Peace and satisfaction.   Peace and quiet. Strange souls are abounding. The Universe is beset with genius. Let me share some of mine.

<u>Believing</u>

I had a transporter moment today. A Shaman moment.
A visit to another world. I was sitting in the break room,
peeling an orange. I was doing the Bear thing where I sniffed
the peel, and slowly ate it. Savored it. Taking over an hour to
accomplish the task.

I closed my eyes and was transported to a cafe with
Sudah, Roz, Augusta and me taking up a booth. It was like the
red vinyl booths at Reyna's but it was not Reyna's because we
were not eating chips and salsa. Although it could have been
Reyna's and we were all abstaining. Augusta asked me if I
believed in God. In response I closed my eyes and continued
to peel the orange all over again. I talked about how that
orange reminds me of summer days. Of me and my brother
and a group of friends climbing into the bed of the grey
growler and doing the fifteen kids in the back of a
paddywagon thing, cruising down to the lake. It reminded me
of reaching out the side of the truck and grabbing hold of tree
limbs that were encroaching on the side of the road. Trying to
pull them off. Trying to make that satisfying snapping of
branches sound. But usually only getting a handful of wet,
green, crushed leaves in your fist. It reminded me of how
Jason would always take the last of everything we had,
whenever we would have something good in the house.
Popsicles, Otter pops, Fudgesicles, Drumsticks, (you can see
we had a well stocked larders) even things that were nasty
like Smarties or Tootsie Rolls he would take the last one from

me and shove it into his mouth with a gloating sneer.

One hot August day in the back of the truck on the way to the beach, just him and I, Jason was savoring the last of a box of Nutty Buddies from the freezer. After scarfing the chocolate and nuts straight away, he was rapidly digging at the remaining vanilla ice cream with his tongue. Working his way down to the little blob of chocolate in the bottom tip of the cone as fast as he could. When I casually reached out and grabbed a hold of a baby maple tree and held onto the end of the branch until it catapulted back into position, leaving only a handful of smashed and dewy leaves in my fist. But that Summer, Tent Caterpillars had infested the boughs of many similar trees in our neighborhood. I looked down into my hand and in addition to the crushed foliage a tent worm must have been feasting at the end of the branch I had caught hold of. His green and yellow innards oozed out of his crushed body as he writhed away the last few moments of his short ass life. And with such casualness so as not to require even a hundredth second of thought, I flicked the caterpillar like a wet booger toward my brother, simply for the amusement of watching him panic as it flew toward him.

And that, to answer Augusta's question, is when I knew God existed. Right then and there. Because Jason did not flinch or panic. Instead he froze, with his ice cream cone poised about a foot from his mouth. And in that moment, God came down from Heaven, and cradled my many legged friend in his hands, and though he did not resurrect the vegetarian beast-pest, he did escort him on a perfect path, a pristine arc through the air, Ronald McDonald could not have drawn a more perfect arc as the worm rose and plateaued and fell, right onto the white landing pad of the last Nutty Buddie that Jason was enjoying.

It was divine intervention all the way. I knew it the second that the worm hit the ice cream and stuck, wet green innards oozing in the white melty sticky bulls eye. My brother looked from his cone to me, completely agog. It was something that could not be repeated if I had a hundred do-overs. A thousand do-overs. But somehow it was nailed on attempt number one. Only God knows why.

Of course I expected Jason to retaliate, which he did, by firing his ruined ice cream cone at my torso and leaving a vanilla stain on my shirt and a red welt on my chest. When we got to the swimming area my Dad saw the mess on my shirt and the trip to the beach was cancelled. I begged to go down to the lake and wash off but he yelled and shouted and drove home, way too fast over the speed bumps. Eager to get there and spank our asses raw.

So I guess to answer her question. Sometimes I believe in God. When I am in a fun playful mood. When I see the impossible occur without any effort or ability. When the amazing world comes together in perfect form. But when bad things happen. And the world is too disgusting to even comprehend. When swimming trips to the lake are canceled and children are beaten because of Gods miracles; that is when it is hard to be a believer.

Nuclear Flower Meadow Meltdown

I am ready to die. I could have been eaten by a deer. Or drowned in a mud puddle. Or fallen of the face of the Earth. Gravity ceases to exist but only for the select few. The rest rise and rise. It is a DNA thing. Scientists know how to do this. Not the scientists like a chemist or a mathematician. But like, the old style scientists. The ones who figured out how to communicate without cables, or light or sound, but with inviso-signals. Turning audio signals into video signals. Turning telephone poles into kindling. Balancing the Tower in Pisa for funsies. Can we do this now? Can we transfer power? Soon we will be able to transfer energy this way. Then we will be able to attack without weaponry? It will be all about matter transportation.

That buoy is a lot farther than it looks. What kind of a family does that mean we are going to be?

Maybe I will just, live wherever I want to. Maybe I will just keep this car running, follow the owls.

My name is Yesterday. Thursday?

Crossword maze? Trapped! Find your way out.

Where is the keys to please the beggars cheese in needs. A Deficiency of vitamin C is easy to conceive the breeze that blows across knees until we find the big fat grinder instead of disease.

What was that, a changeup? That is way gone.

Turning this gibberish into gold. Turning magic into straw. Magic into dust. But the thing is, the dust is not really dust. It becomes magic again. Like when Death Valley had all that extra rain. And the whole place went nuclear flower meadow meltdown. All these wild flowers and insects that nobody thought was there just erupted out of the Earth. As if planted years ago by aliens. Or a crash landing meteor of vegetation. No war. No Death Valley. Just Magic. Magic out of dust.

The only war that needs to be fought is the war on imagination.

Imagination created everything. There is no limit. No. Fucking. Limit. There are no rules. There is only chaos-imagination and those who are brave enough to use it.

Like Anne of Green Gables.

Wolf Spider

About a week ago I killed a wolf spider. He was an absolute beast. I am not sure if "Wolf Spider" is the official designation of these animals, but that is what I was taught to call them. This mofo was dark brown, about as big around as a Kennedy half dollar. With the ends of his legs stretching even beyond those borders. You could see the hairs bristling up and down its legs. He was in the bathtub. Just chillin' there. Probably wondering why he could not scale the smooth walls when all of a sudden some dick (that's me) with a wad of toilet paper comes along and tries to go all sickhouse on his ass. At first I thought I could just smash him, but after I brought the cottony weapon of death down hard, (but not hard enough) he bounced up and started to scurry around, alternating directions like a TIE Fighter taking evasive action. I tried a couple of times, once he even grabbed a hold of the paper and tried to crawl around to my fingertips. I am not proud of the high pitched squeal that I did not know was in me as I tossed the paper into the tub and hauled ass out of there. I came back and the spider had moved away from the paper and had taken up residence along the edge. He reverted back to the problem of trying to scale the bathtub walls. I grabbed the wad and in one decisive motion of destruction brought the paper down onto the wolf spider with a loud thud. Leaving only a yellowish wet stain where the spider had once been.

The next day the ants arrived.

Sugar ants at first. Those little black pains in the ass that seem harmless but are just kind of gross. I have dealt with them before so I went to the store for some poison and set it out around the small hole they were crawling out of. It seemed to work well until the next day when the ants had migrated to the kitchen. What the fuck? So I added more poison along the wall where it looked like they were most concentrated. They seemed to fade away, but not long after I laid the poison down, a new breed of ant arrived to take their place.

About a centimeter long, black bottoms with red middle and red heads. These assholes move around like they own the fucking joint. Sugar ants take a while to spread but these just wander all over the house without a care in the world. Looking for who knows what. Anyway they have set up shop where the first batch of sugar ants had been, in the bathroom, and seem to be enjoying the feast of poison like candy. So I ask you this? Did killing the spider have a direct effect on the careful ecosystem of this house? Was he spawn camping at the little hole the ants were trying to use to get inside. I can totally see that happening. He was big enough that was for sure. Just munching and chowing down on ants all day long. Then he gets thirsty and wanders off into the bathtub for a drink. Totally understandable. We all get thirsty sometimes. But then he is spotted by me and I know if my girlfriend sees him she will have a piss. So I smash him. And now, having cut that thread of life, willingly destroyed what I never knew was the guardian of my home, protector of the peace and peace of mind, I get to deal with these new little devils for who knows how long... Nice.

<u>Old Mr. Kjorvstadt</u>
&
<u>Old Mrs. Kniseley</u>

There is a war raging in the seemingly serene confines of Happy Holiday.

Old Mr. Kjorvstadt's yard was the paragon of the epitome of perfection. Not a weed or wildflower or dandelion or blackberry bush to be seen. Big beautiful roses and Rhododendrons and a wall of ivy modeled after Wrigley Field separated his yard from the cul-de-sac of concrete that surrounded him.

Perfectly picked out rock formations, potted plants, perennials and annuals, rivers, fountains, and small trees, each their own island on an ocean of a green lawn that would have rivaled the lawn of any professional in the state.

"Even those rich bastards up at the Safeco Field." Old Mr. Kjorvstadt once said as he watched the Mariners bunt their way to another loss.

He spent all of his spare time and most of his spare money on his yard. "This is an important yard." he would mumble, down on his knees, single handedly attacking an infestation of dandelions from Old Mrs. Kniseley's across the street. "If I let my yard go all to hell everyone will see. And THEN what will they think? Their yards are all on the edge of the street. If their yard looks like hell. Who's to know?"

Old Man Kjorvstadt looked like a re-animated skeleton that was trying to infiltrate the human race and learn our secrets of life. His skin drooped and sagged like a tired, moldy tent. Hanging loose over his skin was his sweatshirt and a pair of grey sweatpants hiked up nearly to his armpits. Ed Grimley would've been proud.

When he wasn't actively eradicating weeds, or mowing, or digging or planning for his next improvement, he moved throughout the day with a high powered spray can, RAID KILLZ BUGZ, and from thirty feet away, zapped any and all insects that gave him a weird feeling, which was all of them to be precise.

"Little bastards." He would snarl as he unloaded half a can onto a pair of earwigs who were connected at the pincers. "No dirty bug sex in this yard." He would snarl as the earwigs lay dead. Floating in a puddle of poison and fading foam.

He never had a problem with bugs until the Yellow Jacket war of '99.

***

Old Mrs. Kniseley has been married 4 times in her long life. Three times she married for "love", whatever that meant. And once, the last time she was married, she married for money.

Marrying for money is not the worst thing anyone ever did. In fact, it might be the most honest move any gal looking to marry can pull off. Especially, on the day when she asked her man to marry her, and when he asked her why, she specifically said that the main reason why was for money, the man laughed and agreed to her proposal.

Her 4th husband was a businessman, an inventor, a writer, and an entrepreneur. From the time he dropped out of high school at age 15 he made and lost and remade several fortunes. He built from nothing, no less than 5 companies, which he sold and moved onto something else. He wrote a best-selling book about following your dreams and selling big called, "More Money Than You Can Spend in Your Life" and went on to travel the globe and to celebrate the one shot we all get at this thing called life.

So when Old Mrs. Kniseley met her 4th husband, she was charmed like most women can be charmed by a rich, attractive, youngish, ball of whoop-tee-doo. They dated for a while and she was taken to restaurants and countries and palaces and places she had never even heard of. They calmed down and eventually bought a house and lived together for a little while.

Old Mrs. Kniseley found she stirred up quite the little scandal when she told her family and friends what she had been up to. Outrage was one way to put it, but she did not mind. She was getting too old and had failed too hard at the whole marriage for love thing to get twisted up in what other people thought. But there was the issue of the money that she was concerned about. She liked her rich boyfriend well enough. She liked his money even better. So when she asked him if they would get married he wanted to know why and she told him straight away.

"I would like to have some of your money when you die."

He burst into laughter. He told her that he had more money than he could spend in his lifetime, in ten lifetimes, and would be honored to give as much of it to her as she wanted, marriage or no marriage.

So they got married. And for 12 years, she lived life as the wife of a rich man, which was pretty good.

Throughout their marriage she was free to do whatever she wanted. She took to organic gardening in the yard. She sold her vegetables and fruits at a discount on the side of the road. Sometimes giving them away just for fun. She watched T.V., read herself to sleep, did crossword puzzles, learned to cook, learned how to differentiate between wild edible mushrooms from the poisonous kinds, learned to raise chickens, wrote a book about an extra special chicken that picked mushrooms and solved mysteries that no publisher would touch. She didn't mind.

Her husband asked her one night if she had ever finished her book. He liked it when she would read unedited parts of it to him in bed. He said that the chicken had real personality. When she told him that yes, she had finished and about the failed attempt at publication, he was tempted to start a publishing company just so she could have her book published and Old Mrs. Kniseley laughed at that idea. She told him that finishing the book, and knowing that he liked to hear parts of her little tale in bed, was good enough for her.

Old Mrs. Kniseley loved all of her husbands, but eventually, she loved her fourth husband the best. He did not mind if she wanted to take a trip to New York by herself. He did not mind if he came home and dinner was not waiting for him in the oven. He did not mind if she wanted to hang around with him or give her opinions on politics, or the weather, or join the Toastmasters of America, or spend a weekend in Vegas playing blackjack, 10000 dollars a hand, or spending her Sundays in the Fall glued to the television watching Seahawks football or going over to Cheney for training camp to see if she could get Dave Krieg's autograph.

She loved Dave Krieg. Mudbone, his teammates called him. Nobody knows why. She loved how hot and cold Dave Krieg was for his entire career. How one game he could throw for 400 yards and 4 touchdowns and no interceptions stirring the Kingdome crowd into an anthill frenzy. And she loved how he could fall back down the very next week. And look like the worst player in the league. 4 for 21 passing, 39 yards, 4 fumbles. 65,000 fans murmuring in their place; talking about things like change and mistakes and future.

Her husband used to watch her reactions to NFL football and smile. One day out of the blue, during one of Dave Krieg's less than stellar performances, she very calmly and without emotion said, "Cheering for Dave Krieg is like cheering for your favorite STD." Her husband laughed. It was the way she said it that was amusing. He could tell that she had been thinking about it for a while. He sat and watched as she carefully turned the T.V. off, turned on a lamp, and began to read Treasure Island.

08-17-10

The Greatest Poker Player Alive in the World... Today

I used to be the greatest poker player in Washington State. I used to be the greatest poker player in The World. I used to be the greatest poker player of all time. But to be the greatest at anything almost always comes with a price. For me the price was temporarily mutating into a trickster, a liar, a skeever, and a thief.

Some of the most wicked men in the history of our planet were also some of the most dominant poker players. Richard Nixon was so good at poker that as a naval officer during WW2, he was able to win enough cash from his fellow soldiers to finance his first campaign for the House of Representatives.

The main philosophy you need to embrace as a poker player is that if you want to be good at it you must acquire an understanding for total selfishness. Learn to take without giving. Using whatever tricks & guile & senses & mathematics you possess to outwit & overwhelm your opponents. I was shocked at first when I realized how good I was at this sinister game.

Once I was in a tournament where at the final table, I was seated next to a man in a wheelchair who was missing both of his legs. People were treating him with kid gloves. Bowing out of pots in which he would raise. Not going after his blinds. The table was down to about 5 players when he goes all in pre-flop. I look down & find A-A in the hole. I called without even a thought, without even flinching. I may have even gone over the top just for effect.

And with everyone at the table cheering him on, encouraging the dealer to help him crack my aces, it wasn't enough. I knocked him out & he slowly scooched his way over to the scorer's table to collect 5th place prize money. All while I stacked up his checks and used them to choke slam the rest of the table on my way to another first place finish. It was not until I was heading home, with more cash in my wallet than I had ever held before, that I realized what I had done. Not once, not even for a second, did I consider laying down those aces. In that moment, recognizing what I had become, I knew that I had won my last poker tournament.

I was a shark. A Monster. A swallower of worlds, of swords, of cups, of wands, of pentacles, of women and men. Without prejudice, without discrimination, without a thought or a second effort this transformation occurred.

"But how do you lay down those aces? It just isn't done." That little justifier in my head yells. And I understand him. I also understand that had I laid down those aces, it would have been my last tournament for sure.

Which it nearly was anyways. I only played in two more tournaments after that. I was the first one knocked out both times. I got the message.

Thinking back to that last night when I was driving home I should have recognized that it was my last real tournament. The remorse I felt for not laying down those aces. For not making the unexpected, human, choice, then acknowledging it, finished me off instantly. But looking back, I wish I had done it. I wish I had laid down those aces. If I was going to go down, I wish I would have gone down doing the humane thing. In the least, it would have made a much better end to this story.

Learning to Tie Water Balloons

Some days I feel like an absolute wreck. Like there is nothing I wouldn't give or do for some peace, for someone to spritz away my problems with the wave of a magic wand, for a few hits of acid, or for an extra thousand dollars. I remember how frustrating it was when I was a little kid and I could not tie up my water balloons. I would stick them under the faucet and let them fill up. Usually too full. Then I would pull them out and because I did not know how to tie the knot, water would either come gushing out all over my shirt, or I would accidently pop the balloon all over myself. Either way it was a loss and I became adverse to water fights not too much longer after that.

But at some point, after an unknown amount of failure, I just figured it out. I was trying to tie off the end when some of the water came out, and as I was able to stem the tide, the balloon I was supposed to tie was easier to handle. I used two fingers to wrap around and the little divot between my index and middle was just convenient enough to slide the tip of the balloon underneath, making a perfect little knot. I heaved my balloon with abandon and hit my friend dead on in the chest. But the balloon ricocheted off and bounced away, rolling down the grass hill like a stone. It was then I learned that if you do not fill the balloon up enough that the structural integrity is too sound and it will not burst upon impact. It was a good reminder. Even when we think we find the answer. There could be another problem that will pop up. So keep trying. Keep trying until you can find that balance between water pressure, and tying the end off, and let the balloon fly high until it crashes down on the street, or in the gravel, or in the grass or on someone's head with a glorious satisfying explosion.

<u>Magwire to Blades</u>

If you work hard and be kind to people, wonderful things will happen, and some of those things will happen to you. - Will Wheaton.

Write your stories Wayno. Write them and own them and show them to the World. Show them to the people you love. Create a brand new Universe.

Wil Wheaton may have made me a believer in Twitter. Just with that one post. Ah well. I thought I had a few things to talk about. I thought I had a place to sit and stay. I thought I had an imagination that was around here somewhere. I had a couple of good lines. One about Dan Magwire. A rip will form in the space time continuum that is going to destroy everything but Dan Magwire's one career touchdown pass to Brian Blades. Or it will transform into a stegosaurus sized pile of steaming Dan Magwire. I love saying Dan Magwire.

Maybe my time is now. My time to leave and make things better for myself. Things are pointing in my direction. The direction of kings and wizards and wandering adventurers. What is it that makes people wander. What is it that makes the world spin one direction? What is it that makes the Jehovah's Witness go from house to house having people slam the doors in their faces. People walk, people talk. People stop. People think about the way to succeed. What will the great adventure be? Will it be a battle fought till the end of time? Will it be the survival of the species? The cries for the end have been coming for a long time. Maybe the moment is arriving. Maybe there is something to breathe about. What would this house look like after management arrives? Something is going to click. Something is going to snap open, spill out, create magic in and around us all. There is so much to enjoy. I will take this vacation and then I will go off to my goals and dreams. I will find the path. I will shake the tree. Listen to the boughs of the Earth. Listen to the quiet of the empty freeway. Follow the fox. Walk. Walk in those shoes. How far can we go?

Conjuring the First Dandelion of the Year? It is in Your Hair

I can write books. I can charm people. I can read Tarot. I can smile and shine. I love this life. I love the way. I live the way. I can dance, and sing, and make music, tell stories, inspire strangers and friends. Inspire them to be something special, to be who they are.

Hitchhike to school every single day for the entire school year? Fuck it. Just do it. Just go for it. If someone thinks it is crazy, too bad I say. I am a believer in something wonderful. I understand that there are many choices to be made about where we go, and, what we are doing, and what we are open to learning.

I would love to hear your story. I would love to show you something new. I would love to challenge you to do something difficult. You get to live your whole life a certain way. You get to mope and to weep and to moan if you want to. Or you can go out there and do something about it. You can make magic work at all times. I am a fan of yours. Are you going to start riding your bike again? Are you going to wish and hope and pray? Are you going to run away? Are you going to fall to pieces? I think you may I think you might, find bloody apple cores tonight.

Jiggity Jig.

Get your shit together. No, this job is more like a pit stop for me. It is like a breath of air, before I go back down into the depths of exploration. I can do anything I want to. I think I will travel around the world. I think I will crown and sew my seeds. I think I will play the Christmas game this year. I think I will find a way to smile at the beautiful people. Tell me something new about yourself.

I have a question for you. Do kids still write and pass notes to each other in high school? Or did technology ruin all that sass?

I have a question for you, do you know about music and dance and theatre and love and faith and imagination and mathematics and science and the first dandelion of the year. It is in your hair, you know? The first dandelion of the year? It is in your hair.

Gardening. Swimming. Making alcohol. Singing Harmony. How many people do you live with?

Can't defend. Fucked up man.

Take me for a ride before we leave.

Where are we going?

For a ride. Before we leave.

Which way do you want to go? You can go left, toward your home, toward what you already know, toward safety, toward your parents and your closets full of clothes and your text messages, and your easy existence.

Or you can go right. You can turn down the road and look at what is coming. You can learn new things, go to places you have never been before, all of the roads of the world open up in that direction, this vehicle can take you to New York, it can take you to Canada, it can take you to a hamburger shop, it can take you to a ferry crossing. One way is easy and knowable. The other way is adventure, and mystery and maybe danger. Take me for a ride, before we leave.

I think you are a genius. For a genius, there is no choice. You just take the best path and never look back. Keep going. Keep looking for something. I am sitting at home.

I once gave a hitchhiker a ride. She was a seventeen year old girl. She got in the car and wanted me to take here as far away from her present destination as possible. I obliged her. She could have asked me to take her home. She could have asked me to take her somewhere for lovie-dovey. Instead she wanted to go somewhere new. Somewhere better. I want to take you somewhere you have never been before. Let's go and check it out. Let's go find something special.

You have to go out into the world. You only get one fucking shot at this thing. You only get one try. Let's make some magic. Shit, I'm after having an idea. Do some crazy shit. Just go for it yo. Just go for something brand stinkin' new.

I bet you are a wizard. What does it mean to be a

wizard? To work magic with the tools you have. Usually your own two hands. Your first kiss. Tell a story people. Share with each other. It is like, nothing goes out, nothing comes in.

If I give you an idea, you will only go as far as I have led you. Be better than what someone else has to give you. Be whatever your imagination can conjure from nothing. Be.

<u>Jupiter Jones</u>

At the inns and taverns of Shackleton the legend of Jupiter J. still flourishes to this day. It is here where people still talk of the accomplishments and "untimely downfall" of the greatest ball player in the history of the game. It is pretty much a consensus that his schoolyard and playground legacy will never be surpassed. But is was that one fateful game when he put on the uniform that makes folks still to this day wonder, "What if?"

There is much rumor and conjecture surrounding the details of the birth of young Jupiter. There is no evidence as far as the community was concerned, of his real mother or father. Although he was raised by the baker, the idea that he issued from the bakers loins was, in their minds, impossible. The baker was short, Jupiter was tall. The baker was round, Jupiter was thin. The baker was grey and balding, Jupiter had thick dark locks. I won't bore you with any more comparisons, although the list does go on.

One time a prominent member of the community once quipped within earshot that Jupiter was more likely to be a visitor from the planet Jupiter than the son of a Baker. The Baker did not mind hearing these comments because he knew the truth. That in spite of the physical differences between him and his son they shared one thing that nobody could see, unless of course they had the courage to look. They shared the same heart.

Throughout the city and surrounding countryside there were not two people with larger capacity for love than the baker and his son. With his benevolent nature and pleasant mannerisms people who have problems or need advice the baker would always be in his bakery for them to confide in.

The Baker

He would knead his dough and bake his bread and listen intently to his patrons concerns. After making sure they had said everything that they needed to, the baker would in turn, respond. Then he would then let them choose any one item in his fine establishment. His only instruction being to eat the chosen treat, be it cinnamon roll, or bagel, or biscuit or whatever they decided on, very slowly. And to think about what had been discussed previously as they did so. When they finished their snack, the answer to their question would be revealed to them.

Many people started to believe that the baker had magical powers. These ideas were perpetuated by most of his regulars. Who in turn would become some of his best friends. The poor loved him best and the baker treated them with as much respect and dignity as if they were kings of all the land. And his favorite, the children, whom he could not resist giving mini sandwiches made on his specialty dinner rolls, whenever they had the urge to stop in.

He enjoyed the children so much and got an immeasurable amount of joy seeing them grow and thrive on the food he built with his own hands that he was soon longing for a child to call his own. Having never been married and seeing the years of his life slowly creep away, the baker would occasionally daydream about leaving his responsibilities to himself and the community behind. In pursuit of satisfying the small restless piece of his soul that ached to be a father.

One day, on the eve of the biggest day of the year in Shackleford, the Harvest Festival, just as the bakery was about to close, a beautiful woman and her two children whom the baker had never seen, entered. The woman explained to the baker that she was with a travelling group of performers that are currently encamped in the forest by the river. And that they unfortunately have run out of food. She makes the offer to gladly overpay the baker after the festival is over, for whatever foodstuffs she is allowed to take back to her camp this evening.

He decides to chat with the woman while considering her proposal. She answers all of his questions honestly. She tells him that her name is Universe and that her son is named Sun and her daughter is named Rain. He wonders what her role is in the group of performers and before he has a chance to ask she gives him his answer. She is The Soothsayer.

The baker hears this and makes the incorrect guess that this means "fortune teller". She tells him that he is partly right; but lets him know that a soothsayers' main focus deals with the truth. These truths can be revealed to people in the past and present as well as in the future.

The baker listened a little bit longer and passed out his

last three raspberry scones from the batch he made that morning. The kids each got a whole one and he cut the third in half and shared it with the woman. He ate it slowly, while thinking about her proposal.

After he finished his scone he told her that he would like to help her with one exception and an additional request that were not in her original idea. The first being that he needed her to promise not to pay him extra for any food purchased. He explained to her that he would not feel right taking advantage of somebody else's inconvenient situation. His request is that he is very interested in "soothsaying" and if she was willing he asked if she would be kind enough to tell him what she can find out about him, by plying her craft.

She bowed low, thanked the baker, and gladly agreed to his terms. She asked if he wanted his reading done now or at the festival. He wanted it right away, so they sat down at the table next to the front window and began. The baker did exactly what he was told. He closed his eyes. He placed his hands on the table with his palms facing up. He breathed in and out deeply three times and relaxed.

He felt the woman's hands come down very lightly on his. The woman made an audible gasping sound as she pulled her hands away. If the baker had his eyes open he would have seen the woman taking the rings off her fingers. First the pinkie and ring fingers on her right hand and the thumb ring on her left. She tried to place her hands on his again and the same quick gasping for air and pulling away. Followed by three more ring removals. She tried again and pulled away one last time taking off the remainder of her rings with one exception. The thin silver band on her left ring finger. This was the only ring on either hand when she finally laid her hands on his and held them there for about 5 seconds.

She lifted her hands off his and pulled her hands up to her chest panting heavily. He opened his eyes and she was staring right at him smiling. He was confused. She assured him she was fine and began to tell him about what she had seen.

In the past she told him she saw the way he gave his unsold bread to homeless and hungry people instead of throwing it away. She saw him giving relationship advice to confused women. She saw him enlightening foolish men. And giving free sandwiches to children. She saw his love for his work and the joy it brings to the world to see a man doing exactly what he was supposed to.

She tells him that in the present even with his joy and happiness she saw the dark spot as well. She saw how he believed that all of the children were, in a way, his children because his creations, his work, his food is inside all of them. And she saw that even though he was very proud of this fact, his own needs are still haunting his soul. And she sees him recognizing that as the days get longer and as he grows older the chances satisfaction get slimmer.

She lets him know that she saw a vivid picture of the future. Which is in itself unusual. She explains to him that she needs his permission if he wants to hear it or not. He wants to know if it is good or bad and she assured him it is good. He agrees and she tells him that a year from this exact day the one worry he has in his mind will disappear forever. He will have everything he has ever wanted. And that his magic number is 5.

She tells him that he is a very unique and special individual. She has never met anyone with such a positive spirit on the inside and that it was a joy to read somebody who was not a teenager trying to impress his girlfriend. Or a depressed housewife wondering why she is so unhappy. She was glad to see the baker was going to get what he wanted.

Fiddlesticks

A man and woman are walking on the beach. The man is out in front, using a long thin piece of driftwood as a walking stick. They are both looking for shells and agates and sea glass. He comes across a wedding proposal. "Will you marry me?" written in the sand. He is amused by this and wants to show it to his girlfriend. Who he likes, mostly because she does not object to him putting his penis inside of her. Anyways when she sees it she leaps with joy and wraps her arms around him, then takes the stick from his hand and writes three letters in the sand. Y-E-S. And his wide eyed open mouthed look screams: fiddlesticks.

<u>Tracy's Tale: written on the train from Portland to Tacoma</u>

Once upon a time there was a beautiful young woman named Tracy. Tracy enjoyed life for the most part, all except for her wicked stepfather who had sharp teeth, purple painted toenails and worked at a cardboard factory.

Sometimes he would come home from work all bitter and dehydrated and ask Tracy to fetch him some water from Brimstone Pond.

"Fetch me some water from Brimstone pond girl! Working at the factory makes me dehydrated! Git!"

And he would swat at Tracy with a coat hanger, which she would evade with well learned skills.

So Tracy, after one such exchange, took her yellow beach bucket down to the pond to get the water. Even though the pond did not smell very good, she loved to sit on the bank of the shore and watch the hummingbirds play chase or maybe weave cats tails into long elaborate braids.

The sun shone bright and hot so to cool off Tracy took her clothes off and slid into the red muddy murk of Brimstone Pond.

This was a very brave thing for Tracy to do because

when she was little her stepfather caught her swimming in the ocean. So, to punish her he held her underneath for a very long time. She can still remember the sound of his muted laughter as she grew more afraid, hot tears stinging her eyes as she gulped mouthfuls of salt and wet, until he pulled her up and snarled at her that if she ever went swimming again she would suffer the same fate as the five dead triplets.

So, as I said before, going into Brimstone pond was a very brave thing to do.

Underneath the water, where everything was pretty, Tracy met a girl and they went a-swimming. Held her breath until finally she died and she left her friend on the other side. Everything was gold. Everything was green. She saw a Sea Monkey King and a Sea Monkey Queen. They fed her Cottage Cheese. Chicken of the Seas. And they sent her on her way with a kiss on the cheek.

But before Tracy left they sang her back to life with their underwater song:

"Oh-la-dee-da-Oooooeeee-cha-cha-"

"Oh-la-la-la-Cha-Cha-Cha-"

"Oh-la-da-da-Oooooooeeeee-cha-cha-"

"Oh-wah-cha-cha-CHA."

Tracy crawled out of the pond and was terrified to see

that the mud and color of the pond had dyed her skin a bright red. She rubbed and rubbed, trying to get the stain off of her flesh. She rolled in the dirt and scrubbed herself with Dandelion seeds, all to no effect. As Tracy was trying to rid herself from the evidence of her underwater adventure, the dreamtime sun rose directly overhead and cast its drowsy spell. Tracy barely had enough time to stagger to the high grass before she laid down to a warm dreamless slumber.

Hours passed by as Tracy slept. Her stepfather yelled and grumbled and threatened to go down and get her. But that would require him to get out of his chair & move away from the television for more than 5 seconds, so it was an idle threat.

The Sun finished its downward arc and after a sunset of the most stunning shades of rotten apple core brown and dirty snow white, the Summer Solstice Full Moon sprang into the evening sky.

Tracy slept while the moon rose higher and higher until directly over her body. Then the combined imaginations of the Moon and the Stars rained down on all the land, covering everything with it's cool glow, including Tracy.

By the time Tracy woke up from the Sun Spell, the moonlight and the starlight had worked their magic. The red stains on Tracy's skin had melted away. And in their place were the reflection of the Moon and the soft glow of the stars, absorbed into Tracy's body & soul for all the world to marvel.

As for the stepfather, without the water from the pond

that Tracy was sent to fetch, he writhed and complained with more bitterness and hatred than usual until his body vanished into dust. He was missed by absolutely nobody.

Channeling the Power of Randy Johnson's Mullet

Today at the bank a truck with its bed filled with firewood, pulling another small trailer, also filled with firewood, backed into my shiny red Saab.

It was one of those moments where I was stepping out of the door after finishing my transaction, checking my receipt and I looked up and this truck was slowly backing out of his spot, straight toward the driver's side of my car. He was about five feet away, but as he continued to move closer and closer I stood transfixed. I did not yell or shout for him to stop. I was fascinated with scientific experiment type amusement as if saying to myself, "I wonder if he is going to hit my car. Let's see how this progresses in a Petri-Dish." And as he crunched the door and threw on his breaks he looked out his side window not at the damage he had done, but instead, right at me.

I stood locking eyes with him for a New York second and waited. He broke eye contact and jerked the steering column, I assumed that he was putting his truck into park, but with a revving and a squealing chirp, like that of a caged parakeet, he had in one motion tossed his automatic transmission into D and lurched forward.

I snapped out of my paralysis and shouted, in my best 12th man voice on third down, "Hey! Stop!"

He did not comply. In fact, he accelerated further. I checked for his license plate and from my angle it was hidden behind the trailer. I looked around as if hoping to find a row of police spikes or a firearm handy to try and stop him. Finding no such device available all appeared lost until, my right hand made a hard fist and the jaggedy edges of my car keys dug into the heel of my hand.

In a flash I materialized into Randy Johnson during his unruly mullet days. I pulled my arm back, took one large step forward and hucked that ring of keys without even a thought as to what the consequences might be.

The keys rose on line, pitched high and wild, hitting the driver's side window dead solid perfect.

The window exploded in a shower of sparkling refracted sunlight. The truck driver hit the gas out of reflex and buckin' bronco'd his way over the speed bump at the end of the bank drivethru. The wood in the back of his truck was tied down, but the wood in the trailer seemed to all rise up out of the bed and hover, appearing to come apart at the seams, before it came back down in a rolling thunderclap of wood on metal. Three chunks managed to escape and they fell to the concrete, pieces of bark flying off like hand grenade shrapnel.

The truck hauled ass out of the parking lot without oven stopping when it came to the state highway and must have belched the echo of flame for all of the racket it caused as it roared off into the distance.

I moved over to where my keys had shattered his window. A small spread of beaded glass shining in the sun like diamonds spread out in the parking lot, gathering in mud puddle pools near the speed bump. The three pieces of firewood had stopped rolling, waiting for their fate to be determined. I stood looking down at the beautiful mess of glass, and wood, and impulse, wondering how I was going to get home now that I had lost my only set of car keys.

Dysfunction in the Library

"Come on, we need to go, Lucky is out in the car waiting for us." the mother says, urgency causing her to use the dog as an excuse to get her nearly impossible to control kids out of the library. They do not move or respond in any way. Thirty seconds pass when a similar plea comes forth.

"Let's go, it is too hot for Lucky to be in the car alone," practically whining with parental dysfunction.

One of her kids, the boy I think, though the voice is high enough to cause speculation, sighs back. "Why? We hate Lucky anyways."

"You do not." The mother retorts, fear warbling somewhere in the larynx.

"We do too." A different child's voice chimes in, double teaming and putting the boots to the parent, "He drools all over the seats..."

"...and smells like shit."

"Tommy!"

"Smells like dog shit."

"Like dead dog shit."

"Yeah, I wish he was dead."

Butterflies in the Crocodile Pond

Magic blossoms in the swamp. The frogmen read the future in the flames of the torchlight. The fireflies disagree with their predictions. Cars drive down the nearby abandoned road and run the toads over with the Frogger sound. Billions of tadpoles are released from the joeys pouch to bake on the smoldering concrete. The butterflies are watched by the crocodiles. They land on flowering yellow lily pads, on sticks floating without motion in the stagnation of the murky waters, on other butterflies. The sound of a flute approaches, a soldier sloshes his way in black boots through the moisture, tootling without a care as the crocodiles vanish beneath the surface, and the butterflies resume their trip across the country.

The Ghost

There is a ghost in my room tonight. He rises up from the wizards table. Sometimes he swirls and plays. But today, the ghost moves slow, like a summer catfish. Chowing down on algae and mud and junk from the bottom of the lake. Not interested in lures, or skewered wriggling worms, or anything that might be trying to draw his attention away from being a catfish. That is this spirit. This spirit that joins me. Hangs out with me. In the dark. In the evening. In the morning. In the bathtub.

Page
87

<u>Lawrence the Giant</u>

Lawrence was exhausted. His body beat down and his head splitting with pain over the events of the previous day, which is no small feat when speaking of a giant. As soon as he arrived home in his one room, 3 wall shack of his own construction, he set his massive club in the corner and lay down on his "bed"; which was actually a pile of rocks, sticks, bushes, bark and hay; and fell instantly into a restless slumber. He began to dream…

He dreamt that he had awoken the next day and the sun was shining and the birds were chirping nearby. Which is very unusual, most birds had learned long ago of Lawrence's domain in the crater of the mountaintop and had learned to stay clear of that spot. Not because of anything he had ever done to a bird. To his knowledge and memory which, to be honest, was limited, he could not ever remember having harmed a bird intentionally. He thought that his reputation as a 'giant' had probably been enough to keep away their singing. Which he typically enjoyed.

So he lay for a while just listening to a treat that he thought was the result of the cool breeze and the bright sun. But after a while the song they sang seemed to become curiously familiar. He noticed, after about the 20th time listening, that it was the same over and over again. He wondered about the creatures and risked a peek to see what they looked like. As soon as he stirred the singing stopped and a horn blew.

The giant sat up abruptly and looked out the opening in his home. At first he could not believe what he saw. There were people! Real life people in his garden and they had loaded one of his giant radishes, which Lawrence simply called 'radishes', onto a small machine that they had parked there. He stood up smiled and laughed out loud with excitement as he took a step towards the garden. The villagers fled in horror looking up and seeing a real life giant towering 312 feet in the air and laughing like a child. Strolling toward them with what must certainly be bad intentions.

But he was not a mean giant this Lawrence. And had no intentions whatsoever other than curiosity. His respect for birds extended towards other animals as well. He liked to observe, and tried to learn about them if he could. He, as a rule, only ate meat when he was starving. In addition, he was also respectful enough to remove the skin and cook the meat, if he were eating anything that he had killed. So when he reached the garden and knelt down to get a better look at the tiny invaders he was amused and amazed.

By now the tiny humans were scattering in every direction. Some were heading toward a grove of nearby trees for shelter. Some found large carrot stalks or cabbage heads to conceal themselves. Some ran down the mountain falling ass over tea-kettle heeding not to the bloody scars or broken bones they received for their desperate attempts to live. A small group of humans stayed near the wheel barrow that contained the giant radish. Cowering down and determined to deliver their bounty to the village, they tried desperately to push the oversized (for the humans) barrow toward the slope of the mountain. No good. They lacked the necessary strength to move it under the weight of the portly piece of produce.

To be honest the vegetable is of little concern to the giant. It's in fact one of his smaller ones this year. What fascinated him was the contraption that the humans brought to carry it home in. He reached down and picked it up, standing up in the process, and sending the last group of humans running to the mountain slope. All except for one. A girl of about 15 years of age, undoubtedly one of the thieves' girlfriends who had come along for the excitement alone, was clutching the edge of the barrow with both hands pulling with all her might when the giant lifted the barrow off the ground. She fell inside with the radish and struggled madly to escape. At about 250 feet from the ground she accomplished her goal and began to freefall to what would be her certain death if it were not for the quick reflexes of the giant. Reaching down and catching her as she fell he turned and headed back to his cabin.

Arriving at his bed he set the small cart on the ground and turned his attention to the girl. Since he caught her in mid-air she had not stopped wiggling around. He held her in his palm and she tried to jump off. He clamped her by the waist between his thumb and forefinger she kicked and wiggled and tried to pry his fingers apart. He set her on the ground and she tried to run. He blocked her path with a wall made from his massive hands. He picked her up by her head and she flailed like a fish on a hook. Not sure what to do next the giant effortlessly lifted the young lady to eye level and with no thought whatsoever quickly slipped her into his mouth.

Her struggling was intensified into panic as she kicked and punched at the inside of the giants mouth. Lawrence was amused. Her attacks were ticklish to him as he turned her over with his tongue and listened to her squeal from within. He used his teeth to tear off her clothes and spit them out. He could taste her flesh. It was like nothing he could have imagined. Salty yet sweet and warm like a summer morning. He turned her over again and again sometimes sucking on her hard like a lollipop sometimes playfully gnawing like a dog on a milkbone. While experimenting, he gradually gets a little bit more rough with her to the point where he accidentally broke her skin. And the Giant tasted, for the first time, the warm, one of a kind tone, of human blood.

At that moment the giant that used to be Lawrence ceased to exist. In his stead a monster was born. His jaws came down fast and hard severing the poor soul in half just above her bellybutton. The sound of bones crunching mixed with her violent death screams and the gushing of blood and guts inside his mouth was a sensation impossible to handle. He began to chew furiously. He destroyed her skull, tore through the epidermal layer and smashed the rest of her skeleton into thousands of pieces. As he swallowed, his eyes widen to their full size, became completely dilated and bloodshot. They ceased to blink. He let out a fierce, violent and bloodthirsty roar that could be heard hundreds of miles away in all directions. His heart rate hastened to 10x its normal pace. His sense of smell magnified to detect the blood of the Englishman over great distances. And his feeble mind, resolute in its only task at hand. To find and devour as many delicious humans as possible.

He leapt up from his bed, and following their intoxicating scent, he began to run toward the village of the vegetable thieves. Wondering how he could not have smelled them before now, he ran with such mania that he lost his balance. The mountainside was too steep to stay upright. So he leaned on his back and slid down the mountain on his rear kicking trees and rocks out of his way with his massive legs and feet.

He was a sight to behold barreling down the mountain toward the village of Cliffton. Most of the townspeople were frightened beyond reckoning. Hiding helplessly in their houses or running for whatever shelter the forest or caves could bring.

This he expected but unlike before, The Monster saw where each of them had run off to and had full intentions of catching every last one of the tasty morsels.

However, in the Monsters lust to quickly bring all of the fleeing townspeople to their eminent doom, he failed to see the three who were not in retreat but were at the edge of town facing him like a stonewall. On the left a man about 2 1/2 feet tall with a white beard, he wore a red pointy Santa cap and blue trousers and coat looking nervous, as though he thought that the people fleeing like mad had the right idea. On the right, on all four legs was a small, blue, bare skinned creature with a pointy face, big ears and a bifurcated tail, sitting silent, looking intense. At last, in the middle a young girl, no more than 8 years old, stood. Her brown hair pulled back into a ponytail. She wore a yellow pullover with a white rabbit on the front. It was filthy. As if not having been washed in months. In her left hand she held a small black cauldron by its handle, dangling down to her shins. In her right hand she had her old pillowcase filled with her belongings tied to the end of a stick, like a hobo.

"Is this going to work?" said Mr. Junsten, the short man on her right.

"Maybe" said Emy as the ground began to quake at their feet.

"So... can I go?" he asked

"No I need you to stay here" she said.

"What for?"

"I don't know... Hold my things!" she said as she thrust her stick and pillowcase into his small chest and reached over with her right hand and set it on top of his head in a gesture of comfort. "Besides, Renaissance said that I had to deliver this cauldron to a 'Lawrence the Giant' do you think this is him?"

At that moment the blue creature sprang up off of the ground and sat on her shoulder.

"Alright, I am going to take that as a yes."

She knelt down, set the cauldron on the ground in front of her, and removed the lid. A loud *BOOM* issued forth and a white light shot straight up into the sky. She stood and took a step back looking at the light then to the giant who was now focused solely on her. The sight of his fury, and the avalanche of falling trees, rocks, and earth in his wake, forced Emy to act. She quickly turned the Cauldron on its side and pointed the beam of light right into the Giants face like a spotlight.

The pure untainted brightness entered into, and scorched, The Monsters brain through his eyes, mouth, nose and ears. All he wanted to do was to close his eyes. He knew if he could get his eyes shut it would all be over. But it felt like someone or something was holding them open. Then with all his might he reached up and began to close his eyes using the strength of his huge hands. He struggled and fought and slid and finally clamped his eyelids down tight between his fingers. In an instant he awoke from his dream.

Lawrence is not inside his three wall house anymore. He's outside and completely naked having torn his only pair of pants to bits during his dream. Not to mention he is partially smashed into the side of a cliff next to his cabin, half covered in rubble. It is still night and the moon's out. The garden is untampered with. After a few moments reconnoitering his thoughts and wits, he comes to realize that he has only experienced a dream. He sighs and buries his head in his hands with the futile hope that maybe he can get a few hours of restful sleep. And that when he wakes up, he holds onto the fools hope that his pants will be back to normal and his headache will have gone away.

<u>Mind</u>

The Humidification was madness. I drove through it like a fat woman's unshaved swampy armpit.

God I love the rain. I love the way the rain falls on Saturday mornings. I love the way it sounds, creeping through the roof and windows like ghosts, like Santa Claus. Free repeaters.

I am a free repeater. I am a hungry ghost. I like to try and pretend like I am not. Which warps me. I don't think like other people. It feels good to be me. It feels good to be free. When I have felt it. When I have felt like everyone else. There is science to consider.

A person who claims to be a writer. He instead transcribes other people's words down on papers. He claims that they are his. Like Biff Tannen. Sneaky Time-Traveler. All panther-like.

Scared of the public bathroom? Scared of the sound of birds? Scared of something, something. Who here fears education? I do, I do. I shun away from my wold mind. From my homeless persons mind. Form my poets' musical mind. From my alien abduction mind. From my go swimming in the freezing ass cold Pacific Ocean on Washington's coast mind.

Go ask for money. See what happens. See what

happens. I want a vacation and a kilt and a date and some ball bearings. Peen hammers. Bust it. Super size it. Like a mini boss. Like an evil doer.

All those different voices…

Tarot Card: The World

Paint the story with your hands. Your voice is the color and the shape. Your treasure, your one thing nobody can take away. Your genius, your imagination, your wonder, your bewilderment.

Use these things to lift up the world. The world is not a huge weight, about to crush a trembling kneed Atlas at any moment. The world is a wiffleball. Light and airy. It soars around the sun with the effort of a child's laughter. It can be tossed with abandon from one person to the next. It can be spun on the tip of your finger like a Globetrotters trick, or clobbered with a big red plastic bat, soaring into the sky and landing with a happy whap on the lawn on the other side of the tennis court fence. It can be used as toy to amuse or annoy a dog or a cat. It is made and it will be unmade in a while. So let's not worry about when it will be no more, but enjoy it while we still can.

Imaginationland: Bedtime Stories

"Alright everyone time for bed."

"Tell us a story Daddy!"

"What story do you want to hear?"

"Tell us how you became our daddy."

"You guys have heard that story a thousand times. Don't you want to hear something else?"

"No! No! We want to hear about Meg and Star and Kaylee and Sweet Briar and Summer Storm. Pleasepleasepleasepleasepleaseplease!!!!"

"Alright, alright, everyone into bed. Let's go." And the five children piled into the large wooden bed. Their father grabbed a stool and sat himself down. He brought a white candle over for effect and placed it on the night stand. "Well, now, let's see. Where should we start?"

"With Meg of course." One of the little voices squeaked out.

"Yes. Of course. Thank you Briar. As you know, Meg was purchased at the foodway. She was between the eggplant and the cantaloupe. The price tag for Meg was $5.00. But I managed to talk Phil, the produce guy, down to a two-dollar bill. Meg hates this story. Not because of the story but because every time we go to market, Briar goes up to Phil and tries to exchange her sister for a better Meg."

"**Or** to get that two dollar bill back." said Briar.

Giggling from beneath the covers. "Shhhh, I'm trying to listen."

"Star was found on the beach on the lowest tide of the year. Her father had been down gathering seaweed, clams and mussels when he noticed a pack of seagulls arguing over a prize lying in the sand. They scattered with much protest as he approached and there, wet and cold sniffling in the surf, covered in starfish, was a little baby girl. He peeled the starfish away, wrapped her in his shirt and carried the child home. He fed her New England clam chowder for her first meal. And to this day it is her favorite thing to eat.

"Kaylee I brought into this world with a dream. I had been up late making candles, and there was a whole bunch of leftover bubbling wax in the cauldron. I fell asleep at my drafting table and in my dream the wax began to shake and shudder. It ached to be free. It yearned to live outside of its mold. A candle rose of its own accord and it grew legs and arms and a head. It filled out into the shape of a young child. In the dream I chased it and chased it, afraid that if someone found out what had happened that there would be trouble for sure. But the little candle child was too fast, and too determined. So I stopped chasing it and it disappeared down the cobblestone streets of my mind forever. Or at least, until I woke up. Because when I did, lying next to the fire which had burned down to low coals, in a puddle of red melted wax, was Kaylee. Snoring away with a smile on her little pink cheeked face.

"The first time we met Sweet Briar, the three of us, Kaylee, Star and Meg were out picking wild berries and diggin' up Indian Potatoes when we heard the screeching howl of a cat, or so we thought, stuck up in a tree. We followed the sound for at least a half an hour before we saw her sitting a thousand feet up an ancient Douglas fir. I went back to the house to get my biggest ladder. Briar began to climb down, slowly, hesitantly, still letting out the occasional wail. I came back and set the ladder up but it was too short. Briar came about ten feet away but could find no purchase to get any closer. We stayed for hours until I finally climbed down and we decided to head out. As we moved away, the sound of a muffled thud came from behind as the young girl leapt and landed in a soft patch of Sweet Brier. She ran full speed at me, climbed into my arms and I carried the newest addition to our kid hoard all the way home.

"It was the Solstice and we had the worst Summer Storm in living memory. The waves from the ocean were teasing the foundation of the cottage. Dire northern winds tried to peel the roof off. Candles refused to stay lit. Rain came down so thick we could have been underwater. Lightening licked the land around us like lizard tongues. Thunder so loud the earth was vibrating us in our beds. The next day the sky was blue and the sunshine was putting things back in order.

But the sounds of the storm raged on. We left the house in search of the strange sound and could see a smoldering patch that had been set alight by a lightning bolt last evening. In the hollowed out trunk of a Madrona tree was a child. His eyes were closed but out of his mouth all at once poured the sounds of the previous evening; the rain, the thunder, the vicious winds. I walked close and slowly placed my hand over the child's mouth. The sounds of the storm ceased immediately, but his eyes flew wide open. They had a bluish white hue, like the color of lightning illuminating the purple evening sky. I took him home, and laid him down to sleep in the crib. He rested for 29 days, and when he woke, we named him Summer Storm. For his breath was wind. And his tears were rain. And his eyes were lightning. And his voice was like the universe exploding into life."

Old Skoo Video Game Quiz

I always thought that someone could make an easy million by making a randomizer on the original Legend of Zelda, the same way they have the randomizer for Adventure on Atari 2600. I have a one idea. It came to me. 8-bit trivia. classic video game trivia. I could compile a ton of questions about old school video games in a Pictionary type format. Maybe even Trivial Pursuit format. Maybe I could make the board aesthetically pleasing. It could have pictures of old characters and stuff on it. Old Nintendo icons for the titles. Double points. Or other ideas. Continue? Maybe it could be like a dungeon crawler. Maybe the game pieces could be classic video game icons ala Monopoly. Pewter pieces. Maybe it can be a Penny Arcade game box. They could put it together. I had the idea to use a slip drive or a mechanical device to create a sound portion of the game. Or I could do arbiter. A person on Instant Messenger to settle disputes. Too funny. This is all stuff that I could use to make the game better. Some is out there. Some is doable.

1. Who is the Hero of Kid Icarus.

2. What is the Contra Code?

3. How many lives the Contra Code give each player?

4. Who is the villain of Kid Icarus?

5. Who is the sassy sexy villain of Battle Toads?

6. Name two of the three Battle Toads.

7. Who is the first stage boss in Kid Nikki?

8. QB _____ were the names of which three starting quarterbacks in Tecmo Super Bowl?

9. Which sports title was the only football game to feature Walter Payton, Steve Largent, Brian Bosworth?

10. Who was the Quarterback for the Cleveland Browns in the Original Tecmo Bowl?

11. Which two teams had three passing plays for the original Tecmo Bowl?

12. If you pass a level in the NES version of Super Mario Brothers with Luigi, what does Toad say?

13. How many rupees can link hold in the original legend of Zelda?

14. How many dungeons are there in the Legend of Zelda?

15. What are the specialty items in the first dungeon of the first Legend of Zelda?

16. What are the specialty items in the Last dungeon of the legend of Zelda?

17. Who was the original spokesman for sports talk football on the Sega Genesis?

18. Bonks Adventure was originally played exclusively on what home console?

19. What were the names of the two dinosaur heroes in Bubble Bobble?

20. How many characters were available to use in the original SNES Mario Kart?

21. What are the colors of the three dragons in Atari's Adventure?

22. How much does the blue ring cost in the Legend of Zelda?

23. "Uh-oh, the truck have started to move." is a quote from which playable character?

24. What is the name of the hero in Adventure Island?

25. Technocop was released on which platform originally?

26. Reggie Jackson, George Brett, Daryl Strawberry and Nolan Ryan were all playable characters in what

classic NES Baseball title?

27. Which of these four teams was not included in Lakers vs. Celtics and the NBA Playoffs? San Antonio, Seattle, Portland, Phoenix

28. Who had the highest batting average in RBI Baseball?

29. What is the starting weapon in Goonies 2?

30. What are the three magical treasures in Kid Icarus?

31. Which game features this quote from a shrewd businessman? ""Ha, Ha, Ha. Thanks a lot!"

32. "Sushi, kamikaze, fujiyama, nipponichi..." Is a quote from which WVBA Champion?

33. What is the name of Little Macs personal trainer?

34. What is Glass Joes W-L record before the first bout in Punch out?

35. Which of these is not a playable team in Double Dribble? Boston L.A. Chicago, New York, Houston.

36. Give yourself a point for each character you can name from T&C surf designs Wood and Water Rage.

37. Who is Sonic the hedgehog's sidekick?

38. Which two role players from Super Mario Bros. became playable characters in Super Mario Bros. 2?

39. Who was the villain in SMB 2?

40. What is the most you can win from the Money making game in Legend of Zelda?

41. What is the name of the most powerful sword in the legend of Zelda?

42. Who is the evil Doctor in Mega Man?

43. Who's mega mans creator?

44. Name as many original Mega Man Bosses as you can. A point for each you can get.

45. Who was the last player on any Tecmo Super Bowl roster to play in an actual NFL game. Jerry Rice, Steve Wisnewski, Jeff Feagles, Vinny Testaverde.

46. Who is the referee in Mike Tyson's Punch out?

47. What two ways can ToeJam and Earl get from level to level?

48. What planet are Toejam and Earl from?

49. How many downs does the offense get to cross mid field or score a touchdown in Cyberball?

50. How many ghosts can you name from Pac-Man?

51. How many broken ladders are there on the first level of arcade Donkey Kong?

52. What arcade basketball game features the teams Natural High, Brawl State and Chicago?

53. Which of these actions in Arch Rivals is legal? Pantsing, goaltending, A punch in the face, All of the above.

54. Which one of these NES games did not require the use of The Zapper? Wild Gunman, Hogan's Alley, The Adventures of Bayou Billy.

55. What color are the 3 viruses in Dr. Mario?

56. What is Karnov's weapon of choice?

57. What is the name of the stolen girl in River City Ransom?

58. What color are the kidnapped girls panties in Double dragon?

59. In Tecmo Super Bowl half time show, what color are the flying cheerleaders panties?

60. Which fruit gives you the 5000 point bonus if you eat it in Pac-Man?

61. What color is Player 2's marble in Marble Madness?

62. What are the characters specialties Super Mario Bros 2?

63. In which game did Yoshi make his Debut appearance?

64. In which game did Wario make his debut appearance?

65. Which animals Ears and tail give Mario the power to fly in SMB 3?

66. What mini game between levels gives you the chance to rack up extra lives in SMB 2?

67. What color Mushroom is the 1up in Super Mario Bros.?

68. How fast do you have to qualify to get the pole position in Pole Position?

69. What are the three monsters names in the original Rampage?

70. In the Atari version of Empire strikes back the game play takes place during which of the scenes of the movie? Escape from Cloud City, Asteroid Field Battle, Dagobaugh System Jedi Training, Invasion of Hoth.

71. How much MONEY is a jackpot in Toejam and Earl?

72. What are the hamburger ingredients in Burger Time?

73. What level is the first egg wave in arcade Joust?

74. How many points do you get for killing the Pterodactyl in Joust?

75. The first event in Track and Field?

76. The final event in Track and Field?

77. What is the starting weapon for the heroes in Rush 'n Attack?

78. What are the names of the two teams in the arcade version of Tecmo Bowl?

79. What are the names of the four playable characters in the arcade version of Tecmo bowl?

80. What is the name of the first criminal you have to capture in APB?

81. On which level does the wizard first appear in Wizard of Wor?

82. On which level does the Worluk appear in Wizard of Wor?

83. How many cubes comprise the pyramid on Qbert level 1?

84. Is it possible to complete the Legend of Zelda with the wooden sword as your primary weapon?

85. Which Zelda game was the first in which link was able to ride a horse?

86. How many Sinibombs does it take to destroy a fully constructed and operational Sinistar?

87. How many sinibombs does your ships bomb bay hold in Sinistar?

88. The Sinsitar has 8 different quotes, give yourself a point for each one you can mimic.

89. What is the maximum amount of fireworks that can detonate upon clearing a stage in Super Mario Bros.?

90. How many points is a single pac pellet worth in the original Pac-Man?

91. How many invaders comprise the armada of Space Invaders?

92. What is the maximum amount of points the Mother Ship is worth in the arcade version of Space Invaders?

93. Who is endowed with the Mongolian Chop and the Karate Kick as specialty moves in the 1986 NES title Pro Wrestling?

94. Where does King Hippo Hail from?   How much does he weigh?

95. What are the five sweet rock tunes that blast during game the game play of SNES Rock and Roll Racing?

96. What are the names of the playable characters in Rock and Roll Racing?

97. What are the names of the villain drivers in Rock and Roll Racing?

98. What are the names of the three Lost Vikings in The Lost Vikings for SNES?

99. Describe in varying degrees of detail the 7 fatalities in the original Mortal Kombat.

Jason, Unleashes Hot Fury!

My arcade memories are mostly connected with my brother. We would play all over the place. In fact he was quite astute at selecting various locations for dinner or shopping centers or even grocery stores that we could spend our time rocking the video games whilst Mom was busy doing grown up stuff. Whatever the heck that was.

The earliest memories I have are of the Pizza Huts. There was one in Puyallup where we would go and while Dad got salad bar, Mom dug around in her purse for quarters that we used to play Galaga together on the sit down machine next to the Reese's Pieces and sticker dispensers. We played and argued about who was next until the main course arrived. Which we would devour as fast as we could to get back to the red hot action; if some other kids had not managed to swipe the machine away during dinner, bastards.

Another of my first memories was the Safeway in the Harbor. Somehow they had two video game machines there, which by today's standards seems like pure insanity. I am sure they got constant teenager complaints about noise, foul language, abuse and all of the other bull that we are getting at the flippin' library. Which most likely led to the eventual termination of these anomalous arcade wonders. In any case, the game that I was most fond of was the original Mario Bros. It was two player at the same time and I had a hard time not being able to grasp the concept of working with my brother as his teammate. First off the immediate task at hand in my 5 year old brain was jumping up and smashing all the POW charges into the nothingness that they so obviously deserved. Plus it was totally awesome. Always an enjoyable adventure which usually netted me two or three really hard punches to the arm. For some reason being able to hit the platform beneath him and fuck him up was an endless source of amusement to me. Resulting in another dose of unrestrained violence. It wasn't so much a lack of teamwork as a lack of understanding. I saw him as my adversary not the little turtles and crabs. This backwards mindset always led him to hog the quarters that Mom passed out and not let me play with him after my original transgressions. Fucker. I guess I figured it was the price I paid for him being older. Still totally unfairs. Oh yeah and he HAD to have Mario I was ALWAYS Luigi.

Anyway so he would play by himself and do much better than I, having pissed away my lives on the first level. He could even get all the way to the ice levels. While he would continue on I was forced to spend my ration of one more quarter on the other game available, Pole Position. He was way better at this than I was as well. He would get past the test map and sometimes even get extended time. I could not even qualify for the race. I would crash at least three times into the signs on the side of the road. Because I thought that the explosion was "cool". Yeah I totally sucked at that game. Way worse than at Mario Bros. I guess I was no good at the steering wheel thing. And besides, at least I could succeed at being a disruptive force in Mario Bros. Whereas on Pole Position it just kind of felt like a waste of money. I am sure Jason agreed.

So once my ration was up I got to stand there and watch Jason play and play and play. See this occurs because his pragmatic older brother mindset kicks in while my space out and screw off younger brother mindset was in full swing. Basically he always was the one who would ask Mom for the money. Then he would get a handful, about two dollars worth, of change from Mom. Too busy to extend the same courtesy to me when I protested why Jason got the precious quarters and I got nothing he was ordered to share. Which of course meant that I got one, MAYBE two coins if I was lucky and he kept the vast majority to himself. Which once led to more complaining and the threat that if I did not stop crying that nobody would get to play. I was not the sharpest kid on the block but I knew enough that threatening to take away coins that I had not received due to the greedy nature of big brothers, was as the French say, le bullshit. So I continued to act up and guess what happened? Jason kicked my ass for getting his quarters taken away because I told on him for not sharing. AND on top of that since he was not distracted by playing games he had no other choice to make the rest of the shopping trip Hell for me. Which left me no option but to be a crying babykins tattletale, making the shopping trip Hell for my Mom. Which is, in his own mind, the reason why his money was taken away in the first place. And not the real reason, which is of course, his own greed. This is the first example I can remember of standing up for what is right. Or at least what I wanted. But you know what, I only remember that happening one time. My quarter rations, when dispensed by my brother, increased after that. And came out even from time to time, albeit rarely. So I guess he must have learned his lesson. What lesson that is I have no idea. Something to do with numerators or something. I never paid attention in math class.

After a few years, which in kid years is more like 6 weeks, Mario Bros. was taken out and I remember feeling crestfallen. "Mom, what happened to Mario Bros? I am crestfallen." I think was my exact quote to her. I am not sure if her disinterest in this cataclysmic shift in my grocery shopping world even registered on her Mom radar. At least there was another machine there to replace it. Super Punch Out. If I thought the other two games were hard this one was a complete fucking mystery to me. As if watching my brother breeze through the first two guys all the way to Bald Bull with ease were not insulting enough. The indignity of getting my face owned off my Glass freakin' Joe every Saturday was enough of an embarrassment to never want to play again. Eventually I understood how to play and I found out how to out maneuver (see: tap the same button over and over again) Glass Joe and onto an even greater challenge. Piston Hurricane. Holy Shit. Even his name was bad ass. Plus he was a digital representation of a black man. I had no shot. The nifty moves of Mr. Hurricane were way out of my league. But Jason never seemed to lose to him. Except once when I was reaching over and tapping some of the buttons while he was playing. Totally screwing up his game without him knowing it. But once I was discovered. Oh man, I was a dead man. That is unless I ran back to Mom and her shopping cart speedy quick. Making him choose between pummeling me worse than Piston had, or losing his twenty five cent pixel induced coma that he was applying to himself in liberal doses.

As Piston Hurricane was to me, Bald Bull was to my brother. Except for one magical Saturday when he somehow, someway, managed to eek out a victory. Then he took on Dragon Chan. Whom neither of us had ever seen before. This dude was bananas. He was all flyin' off the ropes and bustin' drop kicks and shit. Like ultimate fighting the early years. But even crazier than that, Jason miraculously pulled off another win. What the fuck? I think he just became the world heavyweight champion of the universe! All of my hounding, and shame, and jealousy of my brother turned into what... Respect? Admiration? Well lets not go crazy, we will call it less shame. Then some freaking crazy Italian chef suddenly appeared on the screen. Pizza Pasta was what he was calling himself. And at that very moment Mom came barreling around the corner with a cart filled with groceries trying to get us to go with her or be left at the store. Me, not daring to go against the words of the all mighty Mom, fell into compliance. But not Jason. He had a new guy to face on Punch out damn it. So we left the store without him.

Mom was filling up the car with groceries and asked me where my brother was. I said he was playing and started to explain about Dragon Chan and Pizza Pasta. Surprisingly to me she was not interested in this little slice of Punchout history that her very own son was unraveling no more than 150 feet away. She told me to wait in the car. A minute later she returned with a crabby looking Jason in tow. I thought he was in trouble. He got in the car and sat down. I asked him what happened and he did not say. I guess I assumed that Mom and gone in and ruined his magical game of Punchout.

Which would be a travesty that I could totally understand. I never got a chance to ask him what happened until years later. He actually remembered this day and laughed that I remembered too. He said that he had lost and not because Mom had come and got him. He was just taking his time putting his name in the top score slot. He seemed pretty proud of that.

Refracting Faith

Through the door in our hearts and heads and floors.
Falling into a world of treasure and jorb. Every path through
the world but peace leads to 8 different kinds of loneliness.
Spiral down and let yourself fall. I can see myself falling. I can
see myself spiraling downward in dizzying quickening freefall.
Until I land in bliss, joy, something brand new.

How can you not believe in God. You really have to at
some point. They say that God is everywhere all of the time.
This is true enough. I am a believer of this. The Universe is
filled with God. Hu-man and each one of woman's members,
are portions of that Universe that is God. And, at the same
time, we are our own universes in and of ourselves.
Sometimes we intersect with other Universes. Other people.
And after enough time goes by, there is no telling exactly how
people are drawn together.

Your mother is a free soul. She can come and go as she
pleases. She has my full permission to light up the world in
any way she sees fit. She has passed her light onto her kids.
Some of them receive it, some of them deny it. Some people
hover over others and try to hide their light. Some people are
indifferent to the light, like a stone it bounces off and stays
where it lands. And some people will reflect the light, refract
the light, let it bounce off them in a thousand different
directions. Each point then bursting into another thousand,
and in an instant there is a million points of light. A thousand,

thousand, with the simple antennae like reflection out into the cosmos, all tucked within the frame of this atmosphere.

And still in some ways the world continues to be twisted like a filthy wet toe rag. Humanity, mutation in the name of evolution. In the urge to stretch itself outside the realm of nature. Rise and fall of the Machines.

The Lovers Song

So he laid his head in her arms, and she spread her fingers through his hair and sang him a song. It was a sad song of her own making. It had no lyrics or music. Just the tone of her hum. And the spread of her fingers. He closed his eyes and absorbed her sounds and her touch like a bumblebee in a sunflower soaking up sunshine. When she stopped, she spoke in a low whisper. That no one but him could hear.

<u>A Room Full of Maps and Other Things</u>

I sit in the house, above my neighbors' garage, next to the forest by the beach. I am sitting in a black leather chair, reading a novel without a title, author and cover. I am surrounded by piles of books like this one. Some of them have had their covers removed and grafted onto other books. Why would she do this? Maybe because it is better than doing nothing. A victrola stands alone in a corner, records piled up 8 feet high to the roof without album covers or sleeves, teetering as a cool draft slips through the room. There are many pictures around the molding. Pinball posters, movie posters, pictures I have taken, pictures girlfriends have taken, pictures girlfriends daughter's have taken, pictures my family has taken. Sitting on the floor and leaning against the wall I can see the layer of dust settling nicely on the top of each picture frame. I sit and read and the candles burn, the fire dies, the cat watches me, the neighbors' dog lifts his head up off my doormat and watches the cat. The hummingbirds whir outside without interjection. I want to go to the forest. All of the adventure has been taken out of the world. So I disappear into the forest and pretend like I am travelling through an unseen land. A place of mystery, and magic. There are imps, red caps, trolls, wiccan barbarians, stone towers, magic carpets, tapestries (like the one the cat is sitting on) scrolls, parchment, birds that can speak, men that can only growl and grunt like animals. If I only knew where to look. If I could find the hole in the ground that leads to their home. Maybe I can sleep tonight. I need to put the cheese and sourdough and wine back in the treasure chest. But it is padlocked. The man who has the key has run away. I fear he may have died in the night.

Old gigantic maps, maps of dungeons, maps of mountains, maps of forests, maps of unknown worlds, are all plastered to the walls. A roll top desk in the corner is glued open by melted candle wax. An indeterminate number of candles are piled amongst the mess. Scrolls piled high like Clavdivs. Some opened, some burned and nearly unreadable. Three fireplaces are along one wall. Sometimes one or two or three burn all at once, with varying colors of flames. A standing globe of the world before all of the continents began to drift apart sits on an ivory stand in the center of the room. Cracked vases hold brittle bouquets of dead flowers. Unlabeled jars on a shelf filled with mysterious black and yellow powder. Or unidentifiable clear liquids. Ammonia maybe, or Lye. A wondrous collection of new and old rugs spread out on the floor. Connected in a haphazard way like a patchwork quilt. A large tall, hourglass, like the one the wicked witch had in the Wizard of Oz. A Crystal Ball. A tall standing coat rack. Piles and shelves and cases of books. Some clearly marked. Some blank with fuzzy covers, filled with invisible ink. Some   sketchbooks waiting to be honored. Others used and swollen with words and drawings, color and life. No TV. An old timey radio. A laptop computer. One electrical outlet. A nest of quilts and blankets and hay in front of the fires for sleeping. Flat surfaces everywhere to work on magical experiments. Sticks from willow trees in the winter time. Potted cactus unattended and content. A black cat sleeping on the highest cabinet. Broomsticks and mops leaning inside of a closet in the corner. A pot of boiling seafood stew. A velvet pouch containing something. An empty treasure box. The unfinished painting of Elephants frolicking in an enormous Maple tree, stilling on an easel in the corner. The paints are dry. It appears as if it has not been worked on in months. There is dirt and dust everywhere. As if the owner of the home is too busy or important or vacant to brush away the filth that has collected for who knows how long.

I Don't Know Why This is Here

I can sit here and surf the internet. I can go to the store and load up on all kinds of video games I have never heard of. I can write my magic words, which turn into magic books, which turn into a grand fortune, which turns into wonder at my surroundings. I can build myself a castle out of stones and cobbles. I can build myself a castle and then build myself a forest around the castle, then build myself and my place to stay. Dracula did it. He had a castle. He had a place to stay. He had a mirror to look into. Mirrors are cool. Almost as cool as rainbows. And Unicorns. And other stuff. Like beef jerky. May all your dreams flow to you on a bottle rocket made of rainbows and Organic Chicken Wings.

09-17-11

Page of Relativity

To an ant, a strawberry is huge.

To a strawberry, a kid is huge,

To a kid, a grownup is huge

To a grownup a tree is huge

To a tree, a city is huge.

To a city a continent is huge.

To a continent, the Earth is huge.

To Earth, Jupiter is huge,

To Jupiter, the Sun is huge.

To the Sun the Universe is huge.

To the Universe, imagination is huge.

01-07-11

Easy as Cake

Our Assignment was to write the boringest paper possible. Some people really got into it. One kid wrote about how much they hated shop class because it was so boring. One girl wrote about a trip her Dad took her to the tire store on her birthday. Another kid talked about how he used to play Nerf basketball in his living room while watching Supersonics games. Memorizing players then playing the games out in his bedroom any way he wants to. He had more fun with the imagination of playing pretend basketball than playing any video game that is for sure. One girl talked about how boring it was during her monthly visits to her Grandpas house. Video games are boring. They increase boredom. Make you more susceptible. One girl talked about a football game. One girl talked about her boring brother and his stupid computer nerd friends. One guy moped about his dull Christmas Traditions, every year the same thing, over to his grandparent's house Christmas Eve. Same presents. Same lame stories. The story about how his grandfather was cleaning the chimney and the ladder fell, and grappling onto the edge of the fireplace he hollered for his wife to help him. His wife sliding the kitchen window open, clearly agitated from having her soaps interrupted shouts "What!" In all kinds of irritability. Or the night she killed six raccoons with six bullets from her old man's .22. Crackcrackcrackcrackcrackcrack. Six dead raccoons, just like that. Someone called the sheriff because firing a gun is illegal, as is the killing of raccoons. But the officer let her off with a warning. Being that he had raccoons in his attic one winter and they were a real pain to get out. The humane society could not kill them. They were bound by law. Which he thought was a stupid law for sure.

There are worse things than having no money. Having no soul being one of the top. Having no passion. Having no joy. Having no friends. Having no imagination. So use your soul. Use your imagination. Use your joy to make stacks of cash. Easy as cake.

Imaginationland: Exploring Infinity

A man stands in an endless fog. It rises up to his neck, seeming to paint the landscape as far has he can see in its dull green/grey brain matter hues. He teeters on his legs, hidden in the fog, like a man on stilts. His bare feet sit in a, moist, slippery, fleshy, coldness, like a mess of mackerel that has been left out on an Alaskan fishing dock all night. He takes an unconscious step forward, like a sleepwalking one year old on a trampoline, knees bowed and wobbling, about to fall on his face at any moment.

He stumbles forward, thoughtless, through the fog. The kind of fog that would lead wild animals astray, out of their comfort zones, away from the breeders into some cold hell where they can not escape. Invisible terrain suction cupping his footsteps in small hillocks under his feet. Head rising and falling in and out of the fog like a casual grey whale in a motionless sea.

With each step the ground becomes more soggy. His feet sink in deeper with every step. To the ankle, to mid-shin, to the knee, to the thigh.

His head disappears under the fog never to emerge again.

The thought appears in his head like the first human memory, "If everything in the world was the same color?

Would we all be blind?"

Standing under the fog, he holds his hands in front of his face. They are barely discernible from the mist surrounding him. Hardly a shade darker then the grey folds his legs are buried in. More memories appear from the void.

His legs, as he tries to lift them out of the loosening bog, feel like something from his past. Something from his childhood. He does not remember his name but he remembers this as it flashes through his mind.

The red dock at the lake. One side of the dock a cracked diving board wobbles and sticks out like a forked tongue. On the other a waterslide, the color of dirty toilet porcelain, bakes in the sun. If you want to use the slide it is important to remember to splash water up onto the surface so your skin does not stick and scold and blister on the way down.

Jumping into the water, either from the diving board, or sliding down the slide, or from the edge of the dock, you could get enough momentum by placing your hands to your sides and shooting straight down feet first to the bottom. Sometimes you would get stuck in the cold soft mud at the bottom of the lake.

It felt like you were 500 feet below. It felt like you could stay down there forever and search the black coldness of the lake bottom with your feet. Trying to pull treasure out of the mud with your toes. Sometimes forgetting that oxygen is necessary to live.

Imaginationland: Falling Through the Mind of God

I fell through the imagination of God and landed on a big top tent. The roof punctured and as I fell through, my clothes slid off like a rotten banana peel. Mid air, my hands grabbed onto something solid. A long, horizontal pole. The crowd roared in amazement. I held on and dangled naked over the circus side show below.

The trapeze handle broke loose from its safety lock. I dropped until the chains caught and swung me across the length of the tent. I reached the edge of my arc and a woman on a different trapeze was there for me to leap to but I got scared and froze. She grabbed hold of my ankle as I started to slip away from her. I let go of my baton and swung off with my foot in her clutches. She dropped me intentionally with a huge smile, down, down into the safety net. It knocked the wind out of me.

I blinked my eyes and the net vanished. I found myself deep underwater. I swam and swam up to the top of a pool. The water was clear and cold and fresh. The kind of water that is hard to find on The Earth. The kind of water that you are glad to make part of you. Fresh, pure, unbottled, unsullied. The real stuff. Like welcome rain on a schmoldering Summers day. It touches every nerve ending and helps reminds you of your life again. So much pleasure in a billion rain drops. How can we possibly count them all?

Up I swam to the light shining on the surface of the water. Looked like sunlight, which I have not seen in what seems like forever. Coming closer to the surface the phosphorescent sparkles of the deep became less. Then vanished. The brightness of the surface light grew by the second.

I burst out of the water's surface like a champagne cork. A wet hard strip of earth is on one side of a cave. Two large stained glass windows are allowing the light to sparkle through. There is no apparent pattern to the stained glass. No religious symbols or signs of nature. A mish-mash of reds and blues, purples, oranges, yellows, blacks. Cut into unique shapes. Purposely designed to not look like anything in existence. Probably

Approaching the windows the stained glass becomes less opaque, more see through. On the other side a giantess stands and looks down. Next to her, a giant man. The giantess has a huge head of 1980's permed hair, frosted, dirty blonde. She has a handbag and looks like she is dressed to go to a conference on improving workplace communications. Female power suit, pearl necklace, Prada high heels. She has a frown and a downcast expression on her face. She is not crying but dark mascara tear streaks are caked down her face.

Next to her a giant man. Head of kinky white hair. Same downcast expression, although he is not crying. Suspect that he is only sad because the woman next to him expects him to be sad. Dressed like a hobo who has been cleaned up and forced to attend church. His eyes do not share the sadness of the woman's eyes, but contain a different kind of sadness. A sadness of someone who's freedom is so far gone they cannot conceive of what that would look like. Freedom? He hears the word and it's meaning has long been abandoned. Now he does whatever the woman says, whenever she says it, without question. If he were to question, then the yelling would begin. And we can't have the yelling. No we can't. So we must have peace at any price. Even if that price is giving up what makes life worth living.

I want to see what they are looking at. I concentrate on the giantess. I want to see through her eyes. But she fades away to black silhouette. I consider knockin' on the stained glass, but I know if I do, these two giants will drop their quarrel, bite my head off, and put me into one of Mrs. MacGregors pies.

So I turn away from the glass and study the series of green sewer tubes before me. The series of waterslides. Down they go, except one. One goes up. Up like the drive though suction tubes of a bank drive through. Up and deposited where? I peek inside and all of the tubes are shooting out into space. Out into the Universe. But which one to take? I peek again and study the stars. These are old fashioned stars. Old timey. These stars do not screw around, or tell tall stories. They are legit marvels. It is hard to believe that the starlight used to be so bright. Bright enough to lay out under it and get a star tan if you wanted to. Very bright indeed.

Freedom, Own Your Freedom

He did not know how he knew, but in an instant he felt like he could snap his fingers and this obnoxious person would turn into anyone he wants. *Click* Like an old fashioned remote control, the kind we called the "clicker" went off. He is turned into a kid. A child with a lollipop. He eats it without looking around at his surroundings.

Going to the same job, going to the same desk every day for the next thirty years. All so you can retire by the time you are 65 or 70 or later. Absurd.

In the mean time you get more and more normal, more and more stuck, more and more self caged. 90% of people are not doing what they are passionate about anyways. So there is that. It is something people who are in prison tell themselves this. It is not so bad being in prison. Most people feel like they are in prison even though they are technically free.

Online Prison. Matrimonial prison. Domestic Prison. Prison to the Banks. Prison to Political agendas. Prison to the Tele. Prison to the law. Prison to the opposite sex. Prison to their kids. Prison to their jobs. Prison to their fears. Prison to what they want in their hearts. Prison to material things. Prison to God. Prison to not believing that God is not. God is in all of the things he creates. Including you.

Inside out. The world feels inside out. The inside of the prisons has appeared on the outside. Freedom does not exist. Your choices are one group of shitty people's rules or another. Well, doy!

I felt freedom one summer. When I was out on my own. It felt amazing. It was scary at times. It was hard. You have to go get it. Freedom is something you go get. Something you go out and find. Something that is magical. Something that is abundant.

How often do you really feel freedom? When you drive over the speed limit. When you walk around naked. When you get a divorce. When your kids go from being underage to becoming adults. When you quit your job. When you drop out of school. When you make any kind of unexpected choice. When you can read whatever you want. Say whatever you want. Freedom. What is it really? God given right? Man given right? Freedom with restrictions. Freedom to devour people as often as possible. Mentally. Physically. Financially. Freedom to subjugate.

Brushing My Hair at the Beach

I brush my hair about once a month. Usually at the beach. I make a day of it. I will pack up a blanket and a lunch in a cooler, flip-flops, some light piece of fiction, lotion and Speedo and off I will go. I find a nice secluded spot and I will first run my fingers through my hair, again and again, over and over, until all of the tangles are out. Then I pull the special brush usually good for dogs and horses, it is the only thing I can get through this beastly mane. I brush it out until it is straight and smooth as possible. Then I will go into the salt water and splash around for a half hour or so. Just floating on my back, all relaxing like, making sure my hair gets nice and salty. Then I will come out, have lunch, and repeat the process. Hands through the hair, then brush. I will go back into the water for more dunking and swimming and splashing, come out, read for an hour then a third time. Hands, hands, hands, brush, brush, brush. Then I grab all of my stuff, my trash, my blanket, my cooler, my lotion, my Speedo. And I head home completely refreshed. Uninhibited by anything that the people of this world may be interested in doing to block the path of peace.

<u>Celebrate Myth, Embrace Ignorance, Do Not Fret, Explore the World Around You, Find Something You Have Never Seen Before</u>

I love the ideas about exploring the mind. I love the ideas about creating things out of nothing. I love the idea of exploring the rooms of our minds. Our thoughts are in one room. It is hard to get out of that room. Let me show you how to get out of the room and to explore the thirty rooms in the house. Let me show you how to get out of the house and explore the country. Let me show you how to get out of the country and explore the world. Let me show you how to get out of the world and explore the Universe.

Celebrate Myth. Celebrate the things we do not understand. Embrace the wonder and the mystery of not knowing. Embrace the wonder of ignorance. Do not fret. Go out and explore the world around you. Find peace. Find joy. Find something you have never seen before.

The Way a Chicken Learns Things

Farmer Bacons tossed a litter of pink baby rats out onto the lawn. They wiggled, and squirmed in place, trying to yawn and squeak, but making no sound. The chicken came by so slow. So casual. Kind of eyeing them the way a fat man eyes newborn babies. He approached sideways, head bobbing and pecked the pink blobs to bloody shreds the way you and I might unfold every blade of a SWISS army knife. Just to see what the hell all of those gadgets do.

07-22-12

<u>Imaginationland: Picking Up Girls at a Funeral</u>

How are you?

Fine, big beauty said in an unintentionally husky simultaneously sexy voice.

We touched eyes. Big, liquid brown, sparkling like Japanese animation, like Bambi's Mother. As usual I fall in love right away. I smiled and she smiled back.

How are you? Reciprocation. The great facilitator.

Terrible! One of my pets died yesterday.

I'm so sorry. She turned toward me and her eyes widened in sympathy. Pupils grew cause that's what they do. What was his name?

People always think boys have boy pets.

Black. And she was a she.

Was black your cat?

No.

Dog.

No.

Curiosity. What then?

She was my deer.

You had a pet deer.

Yes. I still have a pet deer, a white one. But I used to have two and now Black is gone for good.

What happ--. How did she go?

She was shot with a rifle.

The look she gave me should have ended the world. Somehow, miraculously, we are all still here.

I know. What the hell is wrong with people. She was maybe the most beautiful creature you never got to see, not including White. And now she is gone forever.

I am so sorry for your loss. How did you get deers for pets?

They just appeared outside of my house one day. Like the forest dreamed them. Imagined them into life. Munching my neighbors Roses and Peonies. I sat on the deck eating my vegan Cap'n Crunch and just watched them. Two baby deer. One black, one White. They have been coming back every weekend for like two years.

That is amazing, they keep coming back?

Yeah, in the winter I buy cut flowers and toss them out into the snow. They loved it. They would eat a dozen red roses like they were M&M's. It was awesome.

Where do you live?

The Enchanted Forest.

Really? A wave of skepticism seemed to wash over her. She now radiates with a vibration of anger just beneath the surface.

What's your name?

Haley. What's yours?

Aaron. I held my hand out and she shook it with an extra squeeze. You don't believe me. Do you Haley?

Well...

If you don't believe me, come see for yourself then.

What? Come to the "Enchanted Forest" and watch made up White deer eat cut flowers?

Exactly. But... then I stopped and shrugged. Come or stay or go. If the only way for you to believe is with your own eyes, that is what we must do.

She stood. Thinking for a minute. "What the heck is Vegan Cap'n Crunch?" As if this were as equally as absurd as me living in an enchanted forest.

Just popcorn. Homemade, not out of a microwaveable bag. No salt or butter, with sliced bananas mixed in. She had no opinion on my handcrafted breakfast cereal. Then I asked for her phone number. Which she wrote down on the palm of my hand. Then I said as I began to walk away:

Remember, she only comes on the weekends. I don't know what she does during the week. Probably goes to work, sitting in some shitty cubicle or making coffee at a Tully's. She laughed, I continued: But on the weekends. White will come. And so will you. If you want to see and feel one of the few magical and amazing things left in this world. Before it is destroyed by some asshole with a gun.

04-18-12

Sharing

She lowers herself onto my lap, pulling her black skirt up and around her waist, straddling the doorknob popping up from inside my Lucky Pants. I slide my hands up the thighs of her green Tinkerbell tights. She leans down and places her open mouth across my lips and I take her inside of me. Our tongues dance in my mouth. Dazzling and swirling, playing off of each other like improvisational musicians. Our music lights up the darkness. Shared imagination lets us in.

Different Jobs I have Had

A Wandering Wizard. Adventurer. Writer. Author. Photographer. Forager. Clam Digger. Mushroom Stalker. Song Singer. Snake Slitherer. Guitar Player. Love Maker. Elemental Magnet. Conversational Therapist. Bookmobile Rescuer. Tarot Reader. Paragon of Evolution. Twirling Carnival Magician. Food Sharer. Money Maker. Puget Sound Swimmer. Jelly Dancer. Laugher.

Someone was telling me about how freedom has to be taken. Freedom has to be reached out and grabbed. Jill said this. It was a kind thing to say. I was pleased to hear it.

Try new things. Fail like crazy. Don't be afraid to make mistakes. – Cheryl Richardson

There is so much to own in this world. I am so pleased to be me. I am so pleased to be able to go out into the world this way. To find a place to sit and sleep. To find a place to make a stand. I love this world. I love this life. I hope that we will get a chance to live the good life. I hope I will get a chance to make things happen. Find my way through the wilderness. Look for something fantastic to behold.

The Path of the Butterfly

Your Mom has the kind of mind that likes the round pegs all fitting into the round holes. And the square pegs fitting into the square holes. With sections of purple, and yellow and chartreuse all organized in their proper play areas, all lined up in order from smallest to tallest. She would have been good at organizing kids for their class photographs. Or maintaining an assembly line. Or training members of some paramilitary unit that is always getting its asses kicked.

You have a mind like an overgrown field. There is grass and weeds and flowers. Bugs fly around in the sun. There is some shade from an old oak tree nearby. Sometimes it rains. Sometimes it snows. Sometimes the field is set ablaze. When that happens the foliage is destroyed and in the spring, wild mushrooms pop up. I pick 'em, heat a pan, add some butter and fry 'em. They are delicious.

My mind has no place in this world. My mental instability is akin to that of a religious icon, or a homeless sandwich sign holder or a butterfly on its crooked butterfly journey. It is hard to be yourself when this world is nowhere you want to be.

How did you write this book?

Did you ever have a creative thought? Look, when we were down at the beach, you said you had a great idea. You wanted to smash a bunch of glass and create a like, sea glass factory. It was a good idea. And it was all the better because you shared it with all of us. That made it real. That caused it to breathe in the creative air of the Universe.

Every one of us gets a thousand creative ideas a day. Maybe more. But unless they get acknowledged, unless something is done to encourage growth and spawn creativity, they are going to go back to where they came from. And who knows when they will return. Do this by speaking the ideas aloud. Or, writing them down on a piece of paper, or in a notebook. Draw a picture, or take a photograph, anything to take that creative (snaps fingers) spark and then watch it glow, watch it grow. Breathe life into something that was just conceived. A baby is made in the same way. There was nothing and then, click, all of a sudden there is this creative blessing. If you do nothing, if you refuse to nurture this piece of creativity that you were blessed with, it will go back. It will vanish. And it might never return in your lifetime.

That toothpaste tastes just like candy canes. Doesn't inspire a ton of confidence.

What madness is this?

What mental illness can this be?

Make your life. Make something special. You can do it. You can make worlds turn. You can explode stars. You can be the Genius of Love.

<u>Imaginationland: River</u>

You spawn on a high plateau above a fast flowing river.

A gust of moon wind coaxes you over the edge.

On the way down, a dragonfly teaches you how to breathe fire.

You splash hard, loose your bearings, but a bellyful of snowmelt soothes your soul.

The rapids push you under and the engines of the earth crackle and whir and you learn the language of worms and seeds.

On the surface cold sunshine and warm shade alternate unaccountably.

A religious beaver gives you shelter for one night only.

The next day, a rusted suit of armor shakes his fist and it rattles like an empty spray can.

You chip your tooth on a smoove river boulder.

The tooth chip lands in the river and in a swirl transforms into a white tadpole.

The tadpole swims upstream with purpose and impossible speed.

Resting in a low cave you make squeaky love to a Great White Salmon. For the infinity that follows, this cave will be the mating grounds for a new breed of furry half-dragon, half-thaumaturge, half-salmon people.

It is going to be a fight for your sons and daughters and gnoves.

The dead bodies appear like ghosts in the bathroom as your torch spark begins to fade.

I refuse to lie to you.

Your death, by river, approaches.

It will be worse than cancer, than being boiled by lava, than being mauled by a robotic Wooly Mammoth with a long sword.

But your deeds have been recorded in the annals of Hummingbird song.

And floating down river toward your certain doom, you refuse to wipe that goofy smile off of your face.

01-10-13

Allie's Dream

Here's my dream:

I'm on a plane with a bunch of people from my younger days (April Mitchelson is co-pilot) and we go to land but the runway's in a field, and we have to make a sharp turn as we are landing. The plane starts to tip and it does. We all bail out and I think about grabbing my bag but don't, it's not what you're supposed to do. We all (all the kids) stand there for two minutes, then April smells the plane and says Get back, it's gonna blow!   Run back into the woods, jump, and it blows. Then we're all walking. Sis, Syd, Jess, and I are walking and we hear it's a two day walk to the nearest hut. There are still people, but different people around. I say I wish I would've grabbed my violin because then I could play sad songs and make us lots of money.

The dream starts over and this time I grab my violin. Sis, Syd, Jess, and I (as kids) walk. And we're walking through this field expecting to walk two days and talking about how we'll sleep because we have nothing but our clothes. Then I see a bus and say Hey there's our bus lemme get our stuff outta there.

And all the sudden (well, it was building in the background) we're in a war/militia zone, there are guerilla war fighters around and one is lining up kids I know on their knees and shooting them in the backs of their heads, but it is a pistol that blows air not bullets. I see this and he comes for me. I stand and hold out my hands as he shoots at my face, I feel and realize the power in my hands blocking the air. I grab the pistol with one hand and start turning it to point at him, and he is lowered to the ground and then I shoot him. I stand there and I hear cheering and applause or yells of thanks or something and I stand there stoic about to cry.

I go back to the bus and get on, our stuff is there, but I see the bus driver. A beautiful 100 year old woman, all wrinkled with a short white bob. I sit with her. Syd, Jess, & Sis are outside the door non-verbally saying when are you gonna get our stuff. The old woman has a rosary, and then I do too. A young woman sitting behind us tells me the woman has Janis Joplin's rosary, as if I should want it. I think about wanting to take it but it's not right, it won't work. My rosary has two beads that have to do with money on it. The driver and I talk, and touch rosaries twice. She is like Mother Teresa. I turn around and three people in beautiful black & white beaded burkas attempt to board the bus, and I ask if they come in peace. One says no, another looks as if no, so I turn them away. I knew they'd be roughing people up in the bus. Two more show up and I ask again, this time they say yes, I let them on but I'll be watching them, all 5 are on there.

I turn back to the Mother and she looks so tired. I embrace her and hold her and sing to her: Mother, are you alright? Mother, are you OK? Can you still see me tonight? (Can you still hear me tonight?) Everything around us fades into whiteness and we are surrounded by quiet and calm, and I'm holding her, I know she's going deaf and blind and she's going.

Then my alarm goes off.

I want to cry, so I do.   I want to be there with her.

Dreamt on January 10th 2013 in the morning.

02-20-13

<u>Aaron's Dream</u>

I was sitting in some kind of office. At some kind of desk. Wearing the clothes of some kind of white collar office worker. The desk, covered with papers that I had somehow become responsible for. It was midday but it looked like early evening because the dark Washington clouds were doing the space alien hovercraft thing, gushing waterfalls of rain, Puget Sound style. Across the busy street, I could see, in the driveway of an old bungalow, a little girl wearing a left boot on each foot, one sky blue, one pink with black whales on it, frolicking around in the collected mud puddle that had built up in the driveway. She was making big lumbering exaggerated T-Rex marching band stomping circles. Then she switched to high bunny hops coming down with the massive two-footed splash. Blasting muddy water up over her head with squeals and spins and smiles. Her dirty blond hair pulled back into a messy ponytail and her classic yellow rain slicker, unbuttoned, swished and fanned out as she moved like a princess cape.

I turned away for a moment. In the white office. Surrounded by other oblivious white people. In our little cubicle prisons. With our perfect 72 degree temperature and soundproof technologically advanced roofing system, designed to keep what should be the pitter pattering of the rain from even registering in our easily distractible eardrums. I could not help but look back out the window. I sat transfixed by this waterlogged pixie. This genius of joy and weather. She would run back and forth through the puddle, or stand in the middle of the ankle deep water, head pointed skyward, eyes closed, mouth agape and tongue stretched out as far as it could go, drinking in as many drops as she could. I am not sure how I knew, but through the unpredictable sorcery of dreams, I was endowed with the knowledge that this little girl was Allie Denzler. And that as I watched this 8 year old version of her drink in the falling drops of rain, I knew in that moment, that if I did not leave the office. If I did not escape into her world, I would be doomed to slip and spend eternity perpetually falling backward into the void.

<u>There are Babes Everywhere</u>

The wheel in the sky stirs the soup.

New stars shine and smile and say, "Hi" to me every day.

Your dag is a trianglehead of genius.

She survived Hurricane Katrina like a banshee.

The juice of the lemon makes your eyes wide and your kisses moist.

"There are babes everywhere"; I can tell you.

Answers to the quiz in Chapter 37

1. PIT
2. Up, up, down, down, left right, left right B – A select start
3. 30
4. Medusa
5. The Dark Queen
6. Rash - Zitz - Pimple
7. Deth Breath
8. QB Bills, QB Browns, QB Eagles
9. Tecmo Bowl
10. Bernie Kosar
11. Miami San Francisco
12. Thank you Mario but our princess is in another castle.
13. 255
14. 8
15. Boomerang and Bow
16. Red Ring, Silver Arrow
17. Joe Montana
18. Turbografx 16
19. Bub and Bob
20. 8
21. Green, Yellow, Red
22. 250 rupies
23. Solid Snake
24. Master Higgins
25. Sega Genesis
26. RBI Baseball
27. Seattle
28. Tony Gwynn .370

29. Yo-yo

30. Arrows, Pegasus Wing, Mirror Shield.

31. "Ha, Ha, Ha, thanks a lot."

32. Piston Honda

33. Doc Louis

34. 1-99

35. Houston

36. Thrilla Gorilla, Cool Cat, Headhunter and Joe Cool

37. Tails

38. Toad and Princess

39. Wart

40. 50

41. Magic Sword

42. Dr.Wily

43. Professor Light or Professor Wright

44. Gutman, Cutman, Electman, Iceman, Bombman, Fireman

45. Jeff Feagles

46. Mario

47. Elevator or falling off the edge of the world.

48. Funk-o-tron.

49. Six

50. Blinky Pinky Inky Clyde

51. Four

52. Arch Rivals

53. All of the above

54. The Adventures of Bayou Billy

55. Blue Yellow Red

56. Fireball

57. Roxy

58. White
59. White
60. Banana
61. Red
62. Luigi – High Jump, Princess – Levitate, Toad – Super Strong, Mario – none
63. Super Mario World
64. Super Mario Land 2: 6 golden coins
65. Raccoon
66. Slot Machine
67. Green
68. 58.5 seconds or faster
69. Liz, Ralph, George
70. Invasion of Hoth
71. 5 bucks
72. Bun, Meat, Lettuce
73. Level 5
74. 1000
75. 100 Meter Dash
76. High Jump
77. Knives
78. Bulldogs and Wildcats
79. Larry, Bob, Eric, Joe
80. Freaky Freddie
81. Level 3
82. Level 2
83. 28
84. Yes
85. Orcana of Time
86. 13
87. 21

88. Beware, I live! - Run, Coward! – Run! Run! Run! - Wroooaaarrrr! - Beware, coward! - I am Sinistar! - I hunger! - I hunger, coward!
89. 6
90. 10
91. 55
92. 300
93. Kin Korn Karn
94. Hippo Island, South Pacific
95. Bad to the Bone, Paranoid, Highway Star, The Peter Gunn Theme, Born to be Wild
96. Snake Sanders, Tarquinn, Jake Badlands, Katarina Lyons, Ivanzypher, Cyberhawk
97. Viper Mackay, Grinder X19, Ragewort, Roadkill Kelly, Butcher Icebone, J.B. Slash, Rip, Shredd
98. Erik, Baleog and Olaf
99. Sub-Zero Spine Rip Out, Scorpion Skull Burn, Johnny Cage Uppercut the Head Off, Raiden Electrocution Hands, Kano Rips out the Beating Heart, Sonja Blade Burning Kiss, Liu Kang Spin Kick Uppercut.

Special Thanks

Special thanks to Lorraine Denzler for letting me use her wonderful watercolors for the cover. Thank you so much.

All chapters are original thoughts, ideas, stories, things, stuffs, from the author's imagination. Except "Allies Dream" which was a dream by Allie Denzler, used with her permission. And the lyrics in "Tracy's Tale", credited to the Canadian 90's all girl band "Cub" from their sweet ass song, "Go Fish".

And thank you to all of the wonderful souls I have met on my journey through this life so far. I will see you all in the future at the place where the sky and water meet.

Ingram Content Group UK Ltd.
Milton Keynes UK
UKHW041033080623
423097UK00001B/15

9 781304 416278